Katia and Tim Carter

Cambridge IGCSE®

Core English as a Second Language

Teacher's Book

CAMBRIDGE
UNIVERSITY PRESS

University Printing House, Cambridge CB2 8BS, United Kingdom

One Liberty Plaza, 20th Floor, New York, NY 10006, USA

477 Williamstown Road, Port Melbourne, VIC 3207, Australia

4843/24, 2nd Floor, Ansari Road, Daryaganj, Delhi – 110002, India

79 Anson Road, #06–04/06, Singapore 079906

Cambridge University Press is part of the University of Cambridge.
It furthers the University's mission by disseminating knowledge in the pursuit of education, learning and research at the highest international levels of excellence.

www.cambridge.org

First published 2015
20 19 18 17 16 15 14 13 12 11 10 9 8 7 6 5

Printed in Great Britain by CPI Group (UK) Ltd, Croydon CR0 4YY

A catalogue record for this publication is available from the British Library

ISBN 978-1-107-51571-0 Paperback

The questions, sample answers and comments that appear in this book were written by the authors.

Contents

Introduction

The Teacher's Book supports the *Cambridge IGCSE® Core English as a Second Language Coursebook*. The Coursebook is designed for core students who are new to Cambridge IGCSE® English as a Second Language and want to develop their English language skills. The main aim of the title is to offer a clear introduction to the skills and language requirements of the core level and comprehensive coverage and thorough practice of these elements. It will also give them the necessary springboard for going on to the extended level Cambridge IGCSE® English as a Second Language, where they will further develop their skills.

The secondary aim of the Coursebook is to increase students' fluency and accuracy through communicative grammar and vocabulary activities, which have been trialled and tested on students in real English as a Second Language classrooms. These grammar and vocabulary activities are fully contextualised and follow receptive skill sections. The language tasks are also personalised so that students find them meaningful when using the target language.

Throughout the book students are encouraged to become more independent learners so that they can continue with their learning process outside the classroom.

The accompanying Coursebook is divided into ten topical chapters. The topics were carefully chosen to provide an engaging and stimulating context for students. Each chapter is made up of skills and language sections. We realise that, in some instances, teachers only get to see their students once or twice a week. For this reason, each section is self-contained which means that sections can be chosen and taught in any order. The practice parts of each section can be set for homework. The more productive parts (e.g. Activate your English sections) can be used in subsequent lessons as revision. This will provide flexibility and enable teachers to target areas that their students need to focus on the most.

We know that time is of the essence for teachers and that is why we wanted to produce a book that could be used in the classroom without any additional materials if the teacher chooses to do so. The lessons are structured so that students are first introduced to a task, then this task is practised, and finally students attempt to produce their own language using the skills and target language they have learnt.

The Teacher's Book itself is designed to cater for teachers of varying levels of experience. Detailed guidance on the activities covered in the Coursebook is provided to enable teachers to exploit the material as effectively as possible. A comprehensive answer key is given for all activities and exercises. In the Language focus sections the answers are accompanied by detailed explanations of the language items presented and tested.

In addition, the following sections provide further support to enhance the learning experience in the classroom:

- Extra ideas – these are practical ideas for the classroom.
- Teaching tips – these provide general advice on how best to help students improve their English language performance.
- Extra activities – these are photocopiable worksheets to use in the classroom to provide further practice of skills or language presented in each unit.

We hope that this *Cambridge IGCSE® Core English as a Second Language* title will provide a positive and stimulating classroom experience for both teachers and students.

Katia and Tim Carter

Chapter 1
People of the world

Reading

Pre-reading activity

This activity can be done with the whole class or in pairs. Draw students' attention to the picture prompts. Use this activity to see how many words related to greetings students know.

Vocabulary 1

Students work in pairs. They look up the meaning of the words they don't know. Then they match them to the correct picture.

PRONUNCIATION
Point out the different pronunciation of 'bow' for a noun (bəʊ) and for a verb (baʊ). For phonemic symbols, go to www.phonemicchart.com

To listen to how the words are meant to sound, go to http://dictionary.cambridge.org and listen to the words being spoken.

Reading: activity 1

Students scan the text for the correct country and the greeting shown in each photo. Check answers with the whole class. Don't elicit any more detail at this point.

Answers:

Photograph 1: rubbing/pressing noses *(New Zealand)*
Photograph 2: kissing *(not mentioned in the text)*
Photograph 3: embracing/hugging *(not mentioned in the text)*
Photograph 4: bowing *(Mongolia, Japan, Thailand)*
Photograph 5: shaking hands *(not mentioned in the text)*
Photograph 6: pressing palms together *(Thailand)*

Vocabulary 2

Students work in two groups, A and B, and guess the meaning of the words from the text in activity 1. Each group looks up four words/phrases in an English dictionary. Monitor and help, if necessary. Then students work in pairs with someone from the other group. They tell each other what the meaning is and answer any questions the other student may have about the vocabulary. Conduct whole class feedback.

Reading: activity 2

Before students read the text again, draw their attention to the Study tip box about improving reading speed. Then ask them to underline the country in each question, or other key words that will help them to locate the information more quickly (e.g. 'kowtow'). Students read the text individually and answer the questions. Students check answers in pairs before checking with the whole class.

Answers:

1 *Any two from:* misjudging the distance … a rather awkward moment … a very sore nose.
2 People wanted to prove that they weren't evil.
3 Trading of pipes AND the exchange of snuffboxes.
4 Foreigners.
5 Demonstrating the strength AND bravery of the tribe.
6 In China, and can be traced back as early as the reign of Emperor Xuan Yuan, whose reign began around 2697 BCE.
7 To indicate the absence of weapons AND to show respect.

TEACHING TIP
It is a good idea to time your students' reading from time to time to prepare them for exam-like conditions.

Speaking activity

Students discuss the questions in small groups. If possible, students of different nationalities should work together. If the whole class is from the same country, students can share their experience in other countries or what they have read/heard.

Project

The research can be done for homework. Students share their findings in class.

Speaking

Speaking: activity 1

This section introduces the students' speaking paper. This activity tests how much students already know about the format of the exam. Students work in small groups and answer the questions. If they do not know the answers, encourage them to guess first. Check answers with the whole class. Award points for each correct answer.

Answers:

1 No, individually.

2 There are four parts: Part A. Welcome, explanation of the format; not timed / Part B. Warm-up; 2–3 minutes / Part C. Topic card handed to the student and preparation; 2–3 minutes / Part D. Conversation; 6–9 minutes.

3 Part A. The teacher welcomes the student and explains the format of the test and what happens in each part. Part B. The teacher asks the student questions about their hobbies, interests, future plans to put them at ease and to find out which topic card would be the most suitable for the student – this part is not assessed. Part C. The teacher selects a topic card and gives the student 2–3 minutes to prepare their ideas. The student can ask questions about unfamiliar vocabulary, or clarification about any of the ideas on the card. No written notes are allowed. Part D. The assessed part. A conversation between the teacher and the student.

4 Part D – the conversation.

5 Mainly hobbies and interests – not assessed.

6 No.

7 2–3 minutes.

8 Yes – see the answer to question 3 for details.

9 No – it is vital that a conversation takes place from the outset; students must not deliver speeches or monologues.

10 No, answers should be expanded and ideas developed.

11 The five ideas should all be covered in the order given on the card. However, it is important that related ideas are added and explored for good development of the conversation.

12 Yes, the teacher should ask supplementary questions about ideas arising from what the student has said. However, the teacher should not stray from the topic and all five ideas need to be covered within the time limit of 6–9 minutes.

TEACHING TIP

Please note that English speaking tests are often recorded.The teacher and the student have a discussion on a certain topic. This topic is printed on a card which contains some ideas to cover during the discussion. These ideas are often arranged in the order of difficulty, usually starting with personal experiences and moving on to more general matters. The last two ideas are normally more abstract to stretch more capable students. It is important for students to know that their general knowledge is not tested. It is their ability to maintain a conversation in English, develop their ideas, and use a wide range of grammatical and lexical structures that they are marked on.

TEACHING TIP

All speaking activities after reading and listening activities in the Coursebook are designed so that they can be used as preparation for speaking tests. These speaking sections can be easily adapted into topic cards by selecting five questions as prompts.

Speaking: activity 2

Working in the same groups as for activity 1, students look at the topic card. Give them 2–3 minutes to discuss what ideas/details they could include in their conversation. Elicit a few ideas from the whole class. You can put a few ideas on the board for later reference.

Speaking: activity 3

Students listen to two recordings. In each recording a student answers the first prompt, 'the last time you helped somebody'. Students decide which student gave better answers and why.

Answer:

Conversation 2 is more successful. The student develops her ideas better by adding examples and more details. She also uses a wide range of expressions.

Speaking: activity 4

Students look at the transcript, Recording 1. Ask them to find examples of how to expand answers. Elicit a few answers from the whole class. Then ask students to look at the Study tip box on developing ideas in a conversation to check if they mentioned all the possible ways.

Speaking: activity 5

Students work in pairs and decide who is going to play the student and who will play the teacher. They should think first what they want to say/ask. They then do the speaking activity using the card on 'Good manners'. When they have finished, ask a few pairs to have their conversation in front of the whole class. Each pair has a conversation about one of the ideas on the card. If possible, record students and analyse their performance with the whole class.

When analysing students' performance, focus on the following aspects:

- range of grammatical structures
- range of vocabulary
- fluency
- development of ideas
- pronunciation and intonation.

Extra activity

Worksheet 1

Discussion game

Students work in small groups. Each group will need a copy of Worksheet 1, a dice and a counter for each student. Students take it in turns to throw the dice. They move their counter onto the correct square and initiate a discussion with the other students based on the prompt question. The first student to reach the finish is the winner.

Alternatively, each student in the class gets one question. Students mingle and interview other classmates. They then report back to the class what the most common answers were.

Listening

Pre-listening activity

Students work in small groups and discuss what they would miss most from their country and why. Check answers with the whole class and compare students' ideas.

Listening: activity 1

Tell students they are going to listen to four short recordings in an exam-type exercise. Ask them to work in pairs and decide whether the statements about the exam-type exercise are **true** or **false**. Check with the whole class and write students' suggestions on the board. Do not correct students' answers at this point. Then ask them to read the instructions and check if they were correct. Go through the students' suggested answers and correct the wrong ones. Elicit why the statements are true or false.

Answers:

1. False *(Students should read the questions before they listen.)*
2. False *(four.)*
3. True
4. False *(Students should only write up to three words.)*
5. True
6. False *(Students should check their answers the second time they listen and complete any answers they missed the first time.)*

Listening: activity 2

Students read through the questions and underline the key words. Draw their attention to the question words, whether there are two details required, etc.

Listening: activity 3

Play the recordings twice before checking the answers with the whole class. If students struggle to identify the answers, refer them to the transcript at the end of the Coursebook and ask them to underline the answers in the text.

Answers:

1. **a** bread and sunshine
   b fish and chips
2. **a** nervous
   b in a café
3. **a** tea with milk
   b lemon AND honey
4. **a** his brother
   b in the morning / before school

TEACHING TIP

Encourage students to keep their answers to the minimum for this type of question. Also, highlight that in some questions, two answers are required for a mark to be given. Numbers are also tested in listening papers. Students need be careful when currency is used. The correct symbol is required (e.g. £ or $). If numbers are recorded in figures, the correct number of zeros is required (e.g. six zeros for a million).

Project

This could be an ongoing project. This project is designed so that students are given further practice in skills and language that have been acquired in this unit.

If there are no foreign students at your school, ask students to research the aspects mentioned for a particular country. The interview could then be done as a role-play. Students take on roles of foreign students and interview each other.

As a follow-up activity, students write a thank you letter to a friend's family. Before students attempt their answers, elicit the audience, style, register and organisation. Students write their answers in class, or for homework.

Features of the letter:

- audience – friend's family
- style – letter
- register – semi-formal (neutral tone)
- organisation – suggest three paragraphs (paragraph 1 – thank the family, paragraph 2 – what students enjoyed, what they have learnt, paragraph 3 – invite the family)

Writing 1

Writing: activity 1

Students skim read the letter individually and answer the question.

Answer:

To give some exciting news, ask her friend to meet and ask for some advice on do's and don'ts.

Writing: activity 2

Students work in pairs, analyse the piece of writing and answer the questions.

Answers:

1. Her friend Fatma.
2. Informal.
3. Four.
4. Paragraph 1 – ask a friend how she is, apologise.
   Paragraph 2 – give some news, arrange to meet.
   Paragraph 3 – ask for advice/help on some social conventions (dos and don'ts).
   Paragraph 4 – let her friend know she'll be in touch and about Julie's photos.
5. Hi Fatma,
6. Lots of love,
7. Yes. 'Will tweet you', instead of 'I'll tweet you' OR 'must rush now', instead of 'I must rush now'.
8. Yes – examples include *they're, I'm, I haven't, there's*, etc.
9. Yes – examples include *meet up, drop me a line, check out*.

> **Extra idea**
>
> While it is useful to introduce students to idioms and phrasal verbs, it is advisable to present them in context. It is also important not to overload students with long lists of idioms and phrasal verbs. Students also need to know that most idioms and phrasal verbs tend to be informal.

Vocabulary 3

Students work in pairs and find the answers in the letter.

Answers:

1. be in touch
2. guess what!
3. a couple of
4. fancy
5. if it's not too much bother …
6. the sights
7. … ask you a favour
8. drop me a line
9. what to watch out for
10. to check out

Writing: activity 3

Planning a piece of writing

The writing can be done for homework, but the planning is better done with the whole class.

The four main points that should be included in the answer are:

- react to the exciting news
- say if you can meet
- give some tips/advice
- say if you saw Julie's pictures and what you thought of them (optional).

Language focus

Giving advice and making suggestions

Analysis

Students work in small groups and analyse the target language. Elicit the correct answers as a whole class.

Answers:

Expressions used to give advice / make suggestions:

1 You should wear something smart.
2 How about going to the cinema tonight?
3 If I were you, I'd buy something small, like flowers or chocolates.
4 You'd better take your shoes off.
5 Why don't you buy her a cake?
6 Always remember to shake hands with people.
8 Resist the temptation to speak during meal times.
9 Avoid talking too loudly on your mobile on public transport.
10 It's a good idea to pay a compliment to the host about their house.

Extra expressions:

7 (used to give an opinion)
11 (used for polite requests)

Verb forms

For answers see the underlined verb forms in the answers above.

> **Extra idea**
> Search the Internet for a few images of various problems (e.g. somebody missing the train) and drill the key structures from this Language focus section before moving on to the exercises OR introduce some problems (e.g. 'I feel so tired today') and ask the whole class to give you some advice. This provides useful controlled practice of the target language for learners and helps them with their confidence before freer practice activities.
>
> If students keep using the same structure in their answers (e.g. *you should*), encourage them to introduce other structures.

Practice

Exercise 1

You can do this as a whole class activity or students can work in pairs first to spot the mistakes. Project the exercise onto the board, if possible. Invite volunteers to correct the mistakes. Encourage peer correction.

Answers:

1 You should to take your shoes of. (2 mistakes) (*You should take your shoes off.*)
2 Before going abroad you'd better reserch some comon social conventions. (3 mistakes) (*Before going abroad, you'd better research some common social conventions.*)
3 Allways remember watching your personal belonggings. (3 mistakes) *(Always remember to watch your personal belongings.)*
4 When you visit london, its a good idea to queu for the bus. (3 mistakes) *(When you visit London, it's a good idea to queue for the bus.)*
5 Avoid to eat food with ur hands. (2 mistakes) *(Avoid eating food with your hands.) Note: emphasise that 'ur' is only acceptable in text messaging and to be aware of other such usage.*
6 Resist temtation to answer the phone when your in the cinema. (3 mistakes) *(Resist the temptation to answer the phone when you're (you are) in the cinema.)*

Exercise 2

Students work in pairs and discuss what advice they would give to the people in each photo. For example, when you are travelling, you should remember to keep your wallet and passport in a secure place OR you should avoid carrying valuable things in your backpack.

This exercise could be done as a role-play too. Check with the whole class.

Answers:

(from the top, clockwise)

Situation - visiting somebody's home; possible problem – not taking your shoes off.

Situation - meeting somebody for the first time; possible problem – wrong form of greeting.

Situation - in the cinema; possible problem – talking on the phone during the film.

Situation – in a restaurant (table manners); possible problem – talking with your mouth full.

Situation – travelling; possible problem – not being careful with belongings and having a wallet stolen.

Situation – using public transport; possible problem – jumping the queue.

Situation – sightseeing; possible problem – getting lost.

Activate your English

Give students a few minutes to write down a few problems (around four or five). Tell them that they don't have to mention any problems that they don't want to talk about and that they can invent some instead. The students then do the role-play. One student explains their problems, and the other gives advice and makes suggestions about how to deal with their problems. When students have finished, they swap roles and do the same again.

As feedback ask some students if they received any really good advice. Alternatively, a few pairs can demonstrate their role-plays. Others have to listen and say what the problem is, what the advice is and whether the person likes the advice.

Writing 2

Writing: activity 1

Writing correction code

Tell your students that if they want to improve their writing, especially the accuracy, they have to correct their own mistakes. For this we use the writing correction code. (Note that for the correction code to work, this needs to be done consistently. If you feel there are too many symbols, you can reduce the code, but make sure you use the same symbols every time.)

First, ask students to guess the meaning of symbols based on the mistakes. Then, check with the whole class and correct the mistakes in the right-hand column.

Answers:

Symbol	Meaning	Example
Sp	*spelling*	I recieved your letter yesterday. *(I received your letter yesterday.)*
WO	*wrong order*	I've been never to Japan. (I've never been to Japan.)
T	*tense*	I never went to New York before. *(I've never been to New York before.)*
WF	*wrong form*	You look beautifully. *(You look beautiful.)*
Gr	*grammar*	He like to 'google' informations. *(He likes to 'google' information.)*
∧	*a missing word*	She said goodbye me and got on train. *(She said goodbye to me and got on the train.)*
/	*extra word used wrongly*	It was too very difficult. *(It was too difficult. OR It was very difficult.)*
( )	*extra word – unnecessary repetition*	He repeated again his answer. *(He repeated his answer.)*
?	*the meaning is unclear*	I how him clean in kitchen with me. *(Nonsensical answer.)*
WW	*wrong word*	I make my homework every day. *(I do my homework every day.)*
R	*register (formal and informal)*	I'm going to get some bread. Moreover, I'm getting my hair done. *(I'm going to get some bread. Plus, I'm getting my hair done.)*
P	*punctuation*	whats your name, im called maria. my brother live's in the uk. *(What's your name? I'm called Maria. My brother lives in the UK.)*
//	*a new paragraph is needed*	... and waving goodbye, she left for California. Many years later, John had a job offer ... *(... and waving goodbye, she left for California. Many years later, John had a job offer ...)*
✓	*Well done!*	I love coming here because I'm really learning a lot and I've made so many friends.

Writing: activity 2

Students work in pairs, decide what type of mistakes they are and then correct them. Check answers with the whole class. If possible, project the text onto the board.

Answers:

Hi Monica,

It was grate ***(WW/Sp - great)*** to hear from you. Hope your exams went OK and you passed with flying colours. I'm so excited that you come ***(T – are coming)*** and can't wait to meet up with you. How could you think that Id ***(P – I'd)*** miss the opportunity to see you?

Anyway, let me tell you what sightseeing we can do together in Prague. I know your time in Prague will be limited because you're going to spend most of the time for ***(WW – with)*** your family, but you definitely must see the historical city centre. It's simply stunning; you've got to see it for yourself. It is quiet ***(WW/Sp - quite)*** small so you can walk everywhere. I think we should walk from Wenceslas square ***(P – Square)*** to Prague Castle and just admire all the beautiful architecture. When you get tired we ***(P – tired, we)*** can always stop in one of the many cafés that is ***(Gr – are)*** scattered along the way and have a cup of coffee. what ***(P – What)*** do you reckon. ***(P – reckon?)*** Let me know what you think.

As for your question about visiting somebody's house, there are sure ***(WW – certain)*** things you have to bare ***(WW/Sp – bear)*** in mind. First of all, remember to take your shoes off. It is very rude if you don't. Also, if I was ***(Gr – were)*** you, I'd get some flowers or box ***(a missing word – a box)*** of chocolates to give to your cousin's family. It's polite to bring a small present when you're visiting somebody for the first time. During diner ***(Sp – dinner)*** you really have to follow a few rules. Even if your ***(WW – you're)*** very hungry, resist the temptation to start eat ***(WF – eating)*** before everybody else is ready to start. Also, remember to say, 'Enjoy your meal' before you start. We don't tend to speak during meal times and be careful to not ***(WO – not to)*** slurp! It is really rude if you do. I think that's it really. If you have any more questions just ***(P – questions, just)*** text me and I be ***(P – I'd be)*** more than happy to help.

Had a look at Julie's photos. They're great. Wish I could go there. Maybe one day.

Take care and see you soon.

Love,

Fatma

Writing: activity 3

Encourage students to rewrite their first drafts of their letters from Writing 1: activity 3, and to correct the mistakes.

Extra idea

It is sometimes discouraging for students to see a lot of corrections in their written work. It is a good idea to agree with your students what you're going to focus on when correcting their work (e.g. week one – spelling, week two – tenses, etc.)

Extra activity

Worksheet 2

Error correction

Use Worksheet 2 for extra practice in proofreading and spotting mistakes. This can be done for homework and checked in the next lesson. At the beginning of the following lesson, students work in teams. Students compare their answers and decide on the corrections together. Then they have a competition. Students give correct answers in turns. To make students more competitive, award points for each correct answer and take points away if a wrong answer is given.

Answers:

1 It's time we went home. / It's time to go home.
2 I'd like some information about trains to Manchester.
3 We are much better at football than them. / We are much better at football than they are.
4 Could you teach me to play the guitar?
5 I'm not very good at tennis.
6 There are a lot of people waiting for the bus.
7 I look forward to seeing you soon.
8 I make a lot of mistakes.
9 Can you tell me where the post office is?
10 I'll phone you as soon as I arrive.

Summary page

Can you remember ...

Students work in teams and agree on the answers together without referring back in the Coursebook. Teams are awarded points if a correct answer is given. Students then assess their own progress.

Alternatively, this can be done as a mini-test.

Answers:

- **four** different types of greetings? *(e.g. bowing, kissing, hugging, rubbing noses, etc.)*
- the traditional greeting in China? *(folding hands)*
- which parts of the body you use when you 'nod' and 'grab'? *(nod – head, shake – hands)*
- how many parts there are in the speaking paper and which one is assessed? *(four parts; only the last part – the conversation – is assessed)*
- what you should do before you listen to the recordings in the listening paper? *(read the questions and highlight the key words)*
- what skimming is? Do you read for detail or for gist? *(quickly reading a piece of text, for gist)*
- if you can leave words out in an informal letter / email? *(yes)*
- what information you can put in the opening and closing paragraphs in an informal letter/email? *(e.g. ask how your friend is, apologise, offer thanks for something in the opening paragraph) (e.g. invite your friend somewhere, give good wishes in the closing paragraph)*
- the phrase that means 'two or three'? *(a couple of)*
- **three** phrases to give advice? *(e.g. 'you should', 'If I were you, I'd',: 'you'd better')*
- what verb form you need in the following phrases?
  'If I were you, I'd ...' *(bare infinitive)*
  'It's a good idea ...' *(infinitive with 'to')*
  'How about ...?'/*(-ing form)*
- what the following correction code symbols mean:
  Sp *(spelling)*
  T *(tense)*
  WF *(wrong form)*
- what the correction code symbol is for a missing word and for a new paragraph? (**∧** and **//**)
- what the mistakes are in the following sentence and what symbols your teacher would use? 'I never have *(WO)* gone *(WW)* in *(WW)* chile *(P)*, but I want go *(Gr/WF)* soon *(WO)* there.' *(I have never been to Chile, but I want to go there soon.)*

Progress check

After completing the Summary page questions, encourage students to go back to the Objectives at the beginning of the chapter and assess their learning progress. Students should use the symbols suggested in the Progress check box. This can be followed up in tutorial time with individual students.

Chapter 1 – Worksheet 1
Discussion game

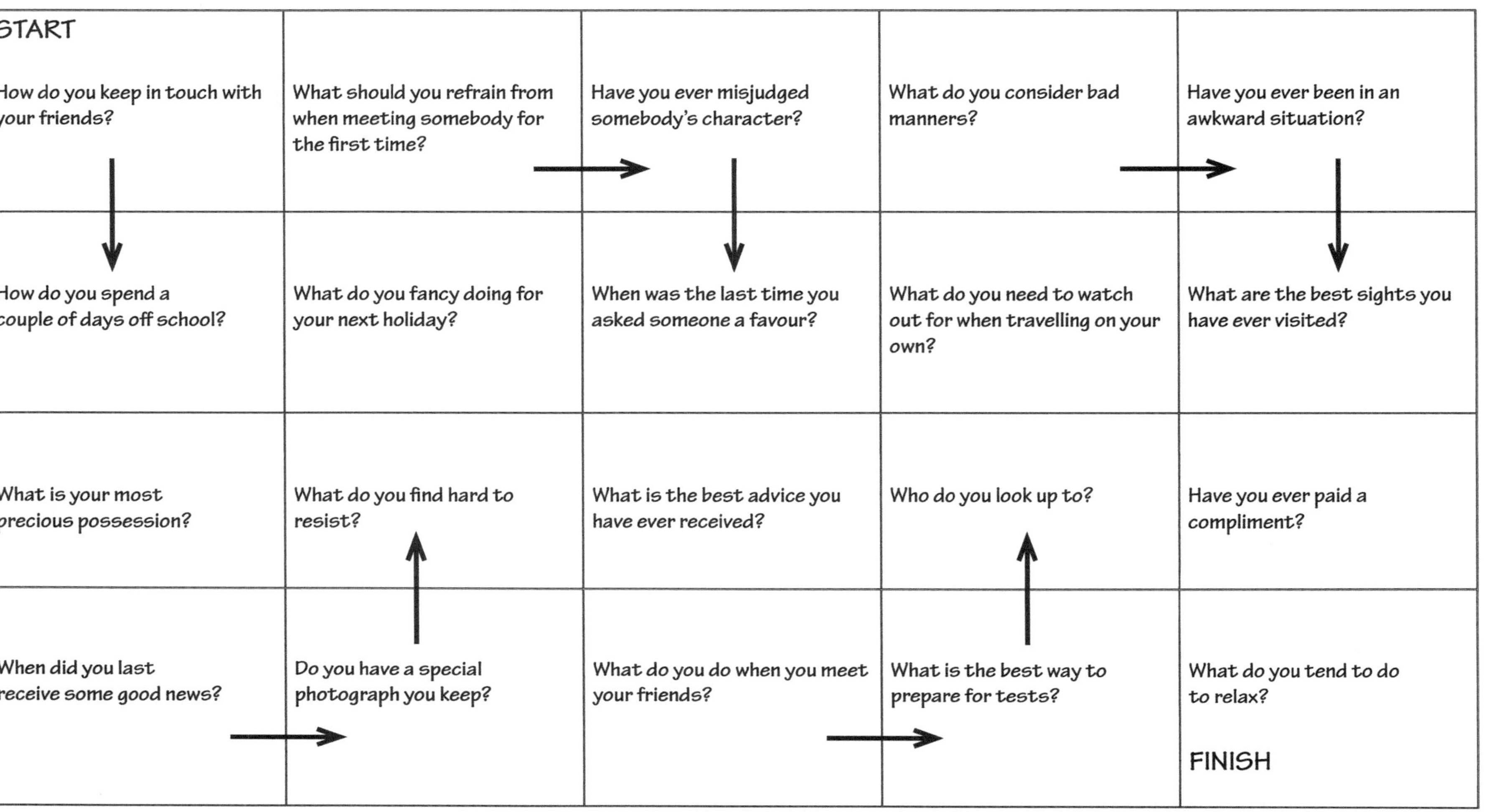

START How do you keep in touch with your friends?	What should you refrain from when meeting somebody for the first time?	Have you ever misjudged somebody's character?	What do you consider bad manners?	Have you ever been in an awkward situation?
How do you spend a couple of days off school?	What do you fancy doing for your next holiday?	When was the last time you asked someone a favour?	What do you need to watch out for when travelling on your own?	What are the best sights you have ever visited?
What is your most precious possession?	What do you find hard to resist?	What is the best advice you have ever received?	Who do you look up to?	Have you ever paid a compliment?
When did you last receive some good news?	Do you have a special photograph you keep?	What do you do when you meet your friends?	What is the best way to prepare for tests?	What do you tend to do to relax? FINISH

Chapter 1 – Worksheet 2
Error correction

Can you correct the mistakes?

1 It's time we go home.

....

2 I'd like an information about trains to Manchester.

....

3 We are much better than they at football.

....

4 Could you learn me to play the guitar?

....

5 I'm not very good in tennis.

....

6 There's a lot of people waiting for the bus.

....

7 I look forward to see you soon.

....

8 I do a lot of mistakes.

....

9 Can you tell me where's the post office?

....

10 I'll phone you as soon as I'll arrive.

....

Chapter 2
Celebrations round the world

Reading

Pre-reading activity

Students look at the pictures and discuss what they think happens at each festival. Then check answers with the whole class. Don't elicit too much detail about the festivals as this is dealt with in the following activities. Focus on the main ideas of each festival. Encourage students to justify their answers.

Reading: activity 1

Divide the class into four groups for a jigsaw reading activity. Each group should read about only one of the festivals and then share the information with the other groups.

Students copy out the table at a larger size, then scan the text for the information required in the table and fill it in. They compare answers in their groups to check that they have the correct details. Monitor and check that each group has the correct answers. Each group nominates one student to give a short talk about the festival using the answers as their notes. Other students listen and fill in the rest of the table. At the end of this activity all students should have information about all the festivals. (For answers see the table below.)

Ask a few questions at the end to check that students have the correct answers. For example: *When is the Mud Festival celebrated?*

Vocabulary

Explain the meaning of 'context' (see the Key term box in the Coursebook). Students work in the same groups as in Reading: activity 1 and look at the highlighted words and phrases in the text. They try to guess the meaning of each word from the context. Demonstrate by using a word or phrase as an example.

For example: 'tend to' – the sentence is, 'In most festivals people <u>tend to</u> put on their best clothes ...'

Explanation: 'people tend to' (it is a verb). 'In most festivals' suggests a frequently repeated action, not one that always happens.

Students should try to guess the meaning of each highlighted word or phrase. Highlight the importance of working out the meaning from the context and go through the Study tip box in the Coursebook. Guessing the meaning of unknown vocabulary is an important skill that students need when reading in both an exam setting or for pleasure.

Answers to Reading activity 1:

Festival	Where	When	Why	What happens
Festival of Colours	India	Springtime	To celebrate the victory of good over evil. To welcome the arrival of spring.	People throw coloured powder paint at each other. They wear old clothes.
Radish Festival	Oaxaca, Mexico	23rd December	To greet the coming Christmas Day.	People carve sculptures out of radishes. There's also a competition for doing this.
Songkran Water Festival	Thailand	Mid-April	To celebrate the traditional New Year.	People throw water at each other. There is also music and dancing in the streets.
Boryeong Mud Festival	Boryeong, South Korea	Between 14th and 24th July	To celebrate the beneficial effects of the local soil (*inference needed here*).	People take part in competitions such as mud wrestling, mud skiing or mud swimming.

Monitor the students while they are doing this activity, but only intervene if the meaning is completely wrong. Do not give students the exact meaning at this point. If necessary, only offer guidance through questions (e.g. *Do you think the meaning is positive? Look at the temperature. Is it high or low? What does it mean for the adjective?*). Students should only use an English dictionary as a last resort.

Check answers with the whole class. Project the text onto the board, if possible. Encourage students to explain how they arrived at the meaning.

Extra idea
It would be useful to have a set of monolingual dictionaries of appropriate level available to the class, if possible.

Reading: activity 2

Students read about all four festivals. This is an exam practice activity. Before checking answers with the whole class, students check their answers in pairs.

Answers:

1. Old clothes.
2. They are the symbol of Christmas in Mexico.
3. Some can weigh up to 3 kg AND some contain intricate details.
4. The radishes are kept fresh by being sprayed with water.
5. It can be unbearably hot; the temperature can reach almost 40 °C.
6. From around Boryeong and it is transported by trucks.
7. The locals and other visitors from outside the city and further afield.

Extra activity

Students could research the meaning of different colours in different cultures. Students work in groups. Each group is given one colour (e.g. red, white) and uses the Internet to research what this colour symbolises in different cultures around the world. They share their findings with the rest of the class.

Worksheet 1

Idiomatic language – colours

This worksheet provides extra practice in vocabulary related to colours.

Students work in groups and look up all the idioms from the worksheet in an English dictionary, or each group can look up one colour only and then share with the whole class. Students work in pairs and make sentences about themselves using the idioms.

For example: 'When it rains a lot, I feel blue.' 'When I feel blue, I tend to chat to friends on Facebook. What about you?'

This activity could also be done as a dictionary race if enough dictionaries are available for each group. The idioms from Worksheet 1 need to be written on or projected onto the board. Each group will need at least one dictionary and a set of cards with the required colours written on them. When students know the correct answer they run to the board to stick the card in the correct gap. The group that uses up most of their cards wins.

Answers:

1. white
2. green
3. red
4. pink
5. blue
6. black
7. green
8. red
9. blue
10. white
11. red
12. blue

Speaking

Students work in groups (different groups from the Reading activity, if possible). Encourage students to expand their answers (see Study tip box in the Coursebook). Do the first question with the whole class to demonstrate how to expand answers. Elicit a few possible answers.

TEACHING TIP
A speaking test is not a knowledge test, but a showcase for the student's language skills. This will improve their development and fluency. Also, if one word, or short answers, are given in English this signals a lack of interest in the conversation and may be regarded as a dismissive or rude attitude by the speaker.

Suggestions for expanding answers include:

- additional information
- personal experience
- comparing with another country
- comparing different time periods, now and in the past
- giving an example.

Project

The preparation for this project can be done either as homework or in class time if Internet access is available. Students can research a festival individually or as a group. Encourage them to look at festivals that are unusual in some way or less well-known celebrations. If necessary, give them a list to choose from.

Also, draw students' attention to language expressions that would improve their talk. Students can also make posters/spidergrams from the outcome of their research for wall display.

After the talk, ask students to write an online review about a local festival they attended. Print out a few online reviews for students to use as a model. Analyse these in class before students attempt their own answers.

Language focus

The passive voice

Analysis

Students work in pairs. Ask them to look at the sentences taken from the texts in the Reading section and answer the questions about the passive voice. Then elicit answers from the whole class.

Answers:

1 In the passive voice we use the auxiliary verb 'to be' (e.g. *is/are*) and the past participle form of the main verb (e.g. *celebrated/thrown/held/known*). Draw students' attention to the Key term box about past participle verb forms.

2 A … was celebrated … B … were thrown … C … was held … D … was known …

Highlight the form of the verb 'to be' in all four sentences and compare these to the first four sentences in the present tense. Elicit that only the verb 'to be' changes when we want to change the tense in the passive voice. The past participle form stays the same.

3 To make comments more general, or to distance yourself from the statement. 'What happens' is the main objective. However, if the agent (the person who performs the action) is required, this can be expressed by adding 'by + agent' (e.g. *The building was designed by a well-known architect.*)

4 It is more common in formal situations (e.g. when writing a formal letter, a report, or in presentations and formal talks).

Tenses

Tell students that you are going to focus on how the verb 'to be' changes in different tenses. Students work in pairs. Ask them to highlight the verbs in each sentence and match them to the correct tense. Encourage students to notice the change in the verb 'to be' in each tense. Check answers with the whole class. Highlight the change in the verb 'to be' for each tense on the board.

Answers:

1 Past simple. Highlight the use of 'was' – the subject 'a letter' and verb 'was' agreement.

2 Future 'will'. This is a future prediction, therefore 'will' is necessary here, not 'going to'.

3 Future 'going to'. This expresses a plan, or an intention, therefore 'going to' is used, not 'will'.

4 Present perfect. Highlight the use of 'have' – the subject 'tickets' and verb 'have' agreement. Note that the passive voice does not occur in the present perfect continuous form.

5 Past simple. Highlight the use of 'were' – the subject 'the photographs' and verb 'were' agreement.

6 Present simple.

7 Present perfect. Highlight the use of 'have' – the subject 'we' and verb 'have' agreement. Tell students that in the spoken form it is more common to use the short form of auxiliary verbs. For example: 'We've' instead of 'We have'. See the pronunciation section on pronunciation of the auxiliary verbs in the passive voice.

PRONUNCIATION

Tell students that sounds often change in English. This is because people link words together. As a result some sounds are shortened, change or are left out. In this section students will practise sounds that shorten and will compare them to sounds that do not change and are strong. The short sound is called a 'schwa'.

Ask students to look at the underlined auxiliary verbs. They listen and answer the questions in pairs. Students listen again and practise repeating the sentences. This can be done as choral or individual drills.

To listen to how the words are meant to sound, go to http://dictionary.cambridge.org and listen to the words being spoken.

> **TEACHING TIP**
> Clear pronunciation is part of the assessment in a speaking test.

Answers:

Weak sounds appear in:
A. Short answers
B. Full sentences✓
(Weak sounds appear in full sentences, i.e. a schwa, because of connected speech. The short answers contain strong sounds, e.g. æ, ɒ, as the auxiliary verbs are not followed by any other words.)

Note that weak sounds are also used in questions.

What is the difference?

1 həz bɪn – weak sound – a schwa.
2 wəz – weak sound – a schwa.
3 wə – weak sound – a schwa.
4 kən – weak sound – a schwa.
5 hæz – strong sound.
6 wɒz – strong sound.
7 wɜː – strong sound.
8 kæn – strong sound.

Practice

Exercise 1

Answers:

1 is cancelled / has been cancelled
2 will be held / is going to be held
3 was … built
4 have … been given
5 is going to be done
6 has been checked / was checked
7 are made / have been made
8 are taken (a fact) / have been taken (one particular test)
9 will … be revealed / is … going to be revealed
10 was spoilt (or spoiled)
11 have been ordered … have been informed

Exercise 2

Students work in pairs or small groups and think of a few sentences for each category. Each pair or group can do one category. Students write their sentences on the board or a large piece of paper. Other students look at these. Encourage peer correction of any mistakes (grammatical, wrong word form, spelling or punctuation).

If time is limited, do one section in class. Students can do the rest for homework.

Activate your English

Students work in small groups. Each student should choose one topic and prepare a short talk. Encourage the use of the passive voice. Give students 2–3 minutes' preparation time. Students give their talk to the rest of the group. Nominate one or two students to give their talk to the whole class. Other students listen and write down examples of the passive voice used by their classmate(s).

Extra activity

Worksheet 2

Verb forms - Noughts and crosses

Students work in pairs and play noughts and crosses with irregular verbs, changing them into the past participle forms. The aim is to change enough verbs to make a line of three in any direction. If the past participle form is correct they can claim the square with either a cross or a nought drawn over it. For example, if the verb is 'choose' the answer should be 'chosen'. If an incorrect answer is given then the student can't claim the square and their partner has a turn. The other student tries to stop the first student or make their own line of three. Set a time limit. The winner is the student with most lines of three correct past participle verb forms.

Alternatively, this worksheet could be used as a board game (a dice and a counter will be required). Students play in pairs. They roll the dice and move their counter onto a square with a verb. Using this verb, they have to make a sentence with the past participle form using the passive voice. For example, if the verb is 'wake', the sentence could be, 'I was woken up by loud thunder in the middle of the night.' If they can't make a sentence, they have to go back to the square they came from and then their partner has a turn.

Running commentary

Find some short footage on YouTube (e.g. how to cook something or how to assemble something) and select the main verbs (e.g. *fillet, season, wrap, slice, grill*, etc.). Give out cards to the students on which they write these verbs. They watch the recording (mute the sound) and put the cards in the same order as in the recording. In pairs they make sentences in the passive voice (e.g. *the fish is being filleted*). Play the muted recording again and students do a running commentary using their sentences. Make sure that the students have enough time to say their sentences – pause the recording if they need more time between each sentence.

Listening

Listening: activity 1

Students listen to Track 5 for gist and answer the questions.

Answers:

- What kind of celebration is she talking about? *(the Rio Carnival)*
- Did she enjoy it? Why? Why not? *(she enjoyed the explosion of colours and sounds and the participants)*

Listening: activity 2

Students work in pairs and predict the answers in each gap. It is a vital exam skill and it also helps students to understand the structure of a sentence in English.

For example: gap A a noun.

TEACHING TIP

Students write one or two words per gap. The word(s) written should be a correct fit for the gap. For example, in gap g) 'respond' would not be accepted as a correct answer for 'response'. If numbers are tested, students need to make sure they use the correct number of zeros. Also, thousands are separated by a comma in English (e.g. 8233 or 1 000 450).

Very often there are distracters in the script to test how students understand the details. To practise listening for detail, students can listen and spot the distracter as a different way of practising this type of exam listening question.

Answers:

A their jobs
B law
C schools
D 2014
E 10 days
F richest
G response
H immigrants

Vocabulary 2

Phrasal verbs and fixed expressions

Students work in two groups and look at Transcript 4. One group looks for phrasal verbs, the other group looks for fixed expressions in the transcript. If the students are unfamiliar with the terms, draw their attention to the two Key term boxes in the Coursebook. Students share the phrasal verbs and fixed expressions they found. Don't explain the meaning to the students at this point. The aim of this exercise is to raise students' awareness of what various fixed expressions are and to give practice in noticing them in the text.

Exercise 1

Students work in pairs and try to match the words they identified in the transcript to their correct definition.

Answers:

1. grow up
2. first-hand
3. out of this world
4. carry on
5. settle on
6. over and over again
7. find out

Activate your English

Students work in groups and discuss the questions using the target language from Exercise 1. Monitor and encourage students to justify their answers. Check answers with the whole class. Then encourage whole class discussion.

Writing

Writing: activity 1

Students read the letter and answer the questions.

Answers:

1. Claire.
2. No, they only have a mutual friend, Claire. Claire wants Aisha to come and meet Mariana to get to know her better.
3. Claire's trip to Switzerland where she met Mariana's family and the trip to the mountains where she had fondue.
4. Persuading Aisha to come to stay with her and to meet her friend Mariana.

Ask a student to read out a few sentences from the letter. Ask others how these sentences sound – very short and simple. The sentences aren't complex; without the inclusion of linkers they sound unnatural / too simple. Elicit the idea that sentences often need something to 'glue them together' to make them sound natural. Also, draw students' attention to the Key term and Study tip boxes in the Coursebook.

Students work in pairs and fill in the linkers. Check answers with the whole class. If time is limited, do the first few gaps in class time and set the rest of the letter for homework.

Writing: activity 2

Answers:

1 but
2 and
3 Anyway
4 because
5 Guess what
6 that
7 since
8 if
9 Then
10 also
11 and as
12 Unfortunately,
13 and
14 while
15 By the way,
16 Another thing
17 because
18 because
19 and
20 and then
21 which
22 so
23 That's why
24 That reminds me,
25 and
26 However,

> **TEACHING TIP**
> While checking answers, draw students' attention to the punctuation (in this case commas) needed with certain linkers. Punctuation is important.

Writing: activity 3

Students select the correct linkers for each category. Then they exchange answers with each other.

Answers:

1 and, also, another thing
2 but, however *Note that 'but' in the letter is used because of 'sorry'. However, allow it as a contrasting linker anyway, as it usually is.)*
3 so, that's why
4 because, and as
5 since, then, and then
6 unfortunately
7 which

Writing: activity 4

Answers:

1 anyway
2 guess what
3 that reminds me, by the way

Alternatively, divide the class into two groups. One group works on Writing: activity 3 and puts the linkers from activity 2 into the correct categories in activity 3. The other group does the same for activity 4. When both groups have finished, they exchange answers. Check answers with the whole class.

Writing: activity 5

Do this activity with the whole class.

Answers:

1 That's why + D
2 and + H
3 By the way, + A
4 However, + E *(Note while 'but' and 'however' have the same meaning, 'but' can't be used here as 'However' starts a new sentence.)*
5 which + F
6 but + B
7 because + C
8 while + G

Linkers with capital letters: *By the way / However / That's why*

Linkers that need a comma: *By the way, / However,*

Writing: activity 6

Students work in pairs. They cover the last column of the table in activity 5 and complete with their own ideas. They use the same linker as in the table in the Coursebook. Students write their sentence on the board. Encourage peer correction and also focus on punctuation.

You will need to cut strips of paper for the following activity. Each pair gets eight strips. Again using the table in activity 5, this time students cover the middle and the last columns. Students can choose a different linker for each sentence in the first column in the table. Using this linker, they complete the rest of each sentence so that it is grammatically correct. It is important that students write only the linker and the second sentence/part-sentence on the strip of paper.

When they have finished, they pass their strips on to the pair next to them. Students match the correct halves to the first sentences in their books. The two pairs check each other's work.

Check answers with the whole class. Nominate a few students to read out some of their second ideas written on the paper. Other students listen and shout out the correct number of the first sentence.

Writing: activity 7

Students write their letters. When marking, focus on content (Are all three points covered?) and linkers.

> **TEACHING TIP**
> Students should practise using linkers and forming complex, natural-sounding sentences.

Summary page

Can you remember …

Answers:

- **one** interesting fact about each of the unusual festivals? *(See texts for details.)*
- where the most famous carnival is? *(Rio de Janeiro)*
- what a popular winter dish in Switzerland is? *(fondue)*
- the name of a mountain in Switzerland? *(the Matterhorn)*
- how to make your talk more interesting for the audience? *(e.g. by including photos, graphs, interesting/shocking facts, etc.)*
- what you should do at the end of your talk? *(invite the audience to ask questions)*
- how to make the passive voice? What two verbs are needed? *(the verb 'to be' and the past participle form of the main verb)*
- what the past participle forms are for these verbs: *buy, choose, find, sing, teach*? *(bought, chosen, found, sung, taught)*
- if the following sentence is correct: 'The students was tell to bring sandwiches for the picnic.' Incorrect: *'The students were told to bring sandwiches for the picnic.')*
- what a phrasal verb is? Can you give three examples? *(See the Key term box in the Coursebook for the definition.)*
- what words are missing from the following fixed expressions: 'experience something first ...', 'do something over and over ...'; 'something is ... this world'? *(hand, again, out of)*
- what complex sentences are? Can you make this sentence complex? 'I went to Shanghai.' *(Complex sentences contain more than one clause. These clauses are often joined together by linkers. Possible answer: 'I went to Shanghai, which is a city in China, and stayed there for a whole week.')*
- why we use linkers? Can you make sentences with these five linkers: 'however'; 'which'; 'that's why'; 'that reminds me'; 'while'? *(To make a text more complex, more natural-sounding. Assess each student's answer.)*
- whether you would use 'furthermore' in a letter to a friend? *(No – too formal, it's the wrong register. 'Also, 'and'* or *'plus' would be more appropriate for an informal letter.)*

Progress check

After completing the Summary page questions, encourage students to go back to the Objectives at the beginning of the chapter and assess their learning progress. Students should use the symbols suggested in the Progress check box. This can be followed up in tutorial time with individual students.

Chapter 2 – Worksheet 1
Idiomatic language – colours

Use an English dictionary and find the missing colours for each idiom.

The colours you will need are:

red, blue, pink, white, black and green

1 to be .... as a sheet

2 to be .... with envy

3 to see ....

4 to be tickled ....

5 out of the ....

6 it was pitch ....

7 to have .... fingers

8 we are in the ....

9 to feel ....

10 to tell a little .... lie

11 to catch somebody ....-handed

12 once in a .... moon

Chapter 2 – Worksheet 2
Verb forms – Noughts and crosses

bite	stick	find	speak	set	know	lend	sell
show	build	tear	eat	leave	shake	keep	steal
tell	fly	break	light	drive	see	throw	hurt
forget	win	lose	burn	ring	drink	hold	teach
wear	freeze	feel	put	buy	hide	draw	send
make	think	give	spoil	go	choose	spend	do
shut	pay	sing	grow	write	take	cut	wake

Chapter 3
The natural environment

Reading

Pre-reading activity

Students work in small groups and tell each other about the places they have visited. Encourage students to cover the ideas in the Coursebook. Tell the students that they can also talk about what they have read; it does not have to be about their first-hand experience. Draw the students' attention to the following points:

- What the place is called.
- Where it is.
- Why it is special or different.
- How they felt when they visited that place.

Reading: activity 1

Before reading, make sure that the students understand the underlined words in the list. Then students tell each other if they know the names of any of the places on the list (e.g. the hottest place on Earth).

Students scan the text for answers.

Answers:

1. Gandom Beriyan in the Lut Desert of Iran
2. the village of Oymyakon in Russia
3. the island group of Tristan de Cunha
4. Mount Chimborazo in Ecuador
5. the Dead Sea

Vocabulary 1

Give out blank strips of paper with the numbers 1–10 to students (one strip per student, or per pair if you want students to look up the meaning in pairs). Give each student, or pair, a word on a separate card to look up. Students look up the meaning in an English dictionary and copy the definition onto the strip of paper. Collect the definitions on strips and put them on the walls around the room (or spread them out onto one desk) for everybody to see. Students match the definitions to the correct word in their book. Check answers with the whole class.

Item number 8 needs to be in the context of 'a scientific base'.

Check the syllable stress for a <u>re</u>cord (n.) and to re<u>cord</u> (v.)

Reading: activity 2

First students read the exam-type question and highlight the important words from the three headings (see the words in bold for answers). Then they read the text and find the correct information to put under each heading. Note that the number of facts needed for each heading is shown by the number of bullet points. This activity could be set for homework.

Answers:

Facts about Mount **Chimborazo** (*any two facts*)

- altitude of 6310 m
- highest mountain above the centre of the Earth
- one degree south of the equator
- 6384 km from the centre of the Earth

Problems of living on the most **isolated** group of **islands** *(any two facts)*

- hereditary complaints / hereditary health issues (asthma, glaucoma)
- no runway on the main island
- it takes a very long time for online orders to arrive

Facts about the Dead **Sea itself** *(any two facts)*

- the salinity (more than ten times that of the Mediterranean Sea)
- the first health retreat
- no life can survive in it

Vocabulary 2

Vocabulary sets and related phrases

Draw students' attention to the Study tip box about vocabulary sets. Explain the importance of this for students' fluency.

Students work in groups. Each group works on one vocabulary set. Note that for 'the coldest place' and 'the most isolated place' there's only one vocabulary item in each category. You may wish to assign these two vocabulary sets to the same group of students to balance the workload. Students read the text again and find words/phrases that are connected with the same topic. The answers could be done as wall posters. Encourage the use of spidergrams to expose students to a different way of recording new vocabulary.

Each group then gives feedback to the other groups. Students can give a short talk about each place to see what information they can remember. Encourage them to use the words and phrases from each word family.

> **Extra idea**
> To extend this activity, students can compete to find out who knows more words connected with the same topics as in Vocabulary 2. Alternatively, you can bring in other topics related to extreme places (e.g. the wettest place, the most populated place, etc.). These extra topics and related vocabulary will be useful for the research project and can be used as a preparation stage in terms of vocabulary.
>
> Give students a time limit of one minute and give them the topic you want them to focus on. Students work together in their groups and try to think of as many words/phrases connected with that topic as they can. When the time is up, ask students to count how many words/phrases they could think of. The group with the most words/phrases reads out their examples. If they are all correct, they get a point.
>
> Alternatively, students can research more related vocabulary for homework.

Project

Extreme places

Students work in small groups and research other extreme places on Earth. This could be a place anywhere in the world, or in their country. If students struggle to think of a place, give some suggestions (e.g. the wettest, the most highly populated, the least densely populated, etc.). This could be in class time or for homework. Draw students' attention to the useful vocabulary provided.

Note that the 'Useful vocabulary' section could also be used after the presentation. For homework, students could write sentences using the phrases and the information they got from each presentation.

Students deliver a short presentation. Promote the use of 'cue cards' and visual materials. Afterwards, encourage 'question' time at the end of each presentation.

After the presentation, ask students to write an email to a group of university students who want to visit the extreme places from students' presentations. Students work in pairs and plan their first draft. Ask them to think about: the audience, style, register, organisation and, appropriate language (if necessary refer students back to the Project in Chapter 1 – giving advice and suggestions). Elicit the answers with the whole class. Students then write an email in class, or for homework.

Features of the email:

- audience – university students
- style – email
- register – semi-formal (students of similar age, but somebody we don't know)
- organisation – suggest four paragraphs (introductory paragraph / how and when to travel, what clothes to take / interesting things to see and do / final paragraph)
- appropriate language – giving advice/suggestions (e.g. *It's a good idea to …*), discuss the opening/closing phrase (*Dear Peter / Kind regards*), the tone should be neutral

Language focus

Comparatives and superlatives

Analysis

Students work in pairs and look at the eight phrases and sentences. They underline all the adjectives and decide if they are in the comparative or superlative form. Draw students' attention to other words surrounding the adjectives (e.g. *more, the*, etc.) to help them decide whether the adjective forms are comparative or superlative. If necessary do this stage with the whole class. Then students answer questions A-J about the target language. Check with the whole class. Ask students for examples for each answer in questions A–J. At the end elicit the comparative and superlative forms for the three irregular adjectives. If necessary encourage the use of dictionaries to find the irregular forms.

Answers:

1 The highest mountain above the centre of the Earth. *(superlative, the … -est)*
2 The most isolated inhabited island group. *(superlative, the most …)*
3 The lowest recorded temperature. *(superlative, the … -est)*
4 The hottest temperature ever recorded on the surface of the Earth. *(superlative, the … -est)*
5 Canada is much bigger than Switzerland. *(comparative, much … -er)*
6 The weather in the summertime is normally a bit better than in the springtime. *(comparative, a bit … -er)*
7 The architecture in Dubai is much more modern than in Paris. *(comparative, much more …)*

8 People in the countryside are said to be a bit friendlier than in the city. *(comparative, a bit … -er)*

Answers:

A Comparative forms use: *'-er' AND more …* *(all sentences 5–8)* / ~~*the '-est' and the most (all sentences 5–8) …*~~

B Superlative forms use: ~~*'-er' AND more…*~~ / *the '-est' and the most … (phrases 1–4)*

C One-syllable adjectives use: *'-er' AND the '-est' (phrases 1, 3, 4 and sentence 5)* ~~*more … AND the most…*~~

D Two-syllable adjectives that end in a consonant + *-y* use: *'-ier' AND the '-iest' (sentence 8)* / ~~*more… AND the most…*~~

E Other adjectives with two or more syllables use: ~~*'-er' AND the '-est'*~~ / *more … AND the most … (phrase 2 and sentence 7) (Note and let students know that there are exceptions to this rule. For more detail, see the 'Rules' below.)*

F Irregular adjectives use: ~~*'-er' AND the '-est' / more … AND the most …*~~ / *different forms from regular adjectives (sentence 6)*

G The definite article 'the' is used with: ~~*the comparative form*~~ / *the superlative form. (all phrases 1-4)*

H The preposition 'than' is used with: *the comparative form (sentences 5-8)* / ~~*the superlative form.*~~

I When we want to describe a small difference between two things, we use: *a bit* (sentences 6 and 8) / ~~*much*~~ *(Note that we can also use 'a little' to express the same idea.)*

J When we want to describe a big difference between two things, we use: ~~*a bit*~~ / *much (sentences 5 and 7) (Note that we can also use 'far' or 'a lot' to express the same idea.)*

Rules:

- When do we use '-er' / the '-est' and when do we use 'more' / 'the most'?

  '-er' / the '-est' is used with:

  One-syllable adjectives (e.g. big)

  Note that one-syllable adjectives that end in 'consonant-vowel-consonant' double their last consonant. Encourage students to use an English dictionary to check the spelling of comparative/superlative forms when in doubt whether a double consonant is needed.

  For example: wet–wetter–wettest / big–bigger–biggest / slim–slimmer–slimmest

  Two-syllable adjectives that end in '–y' (e.g. friendly)

  'more' / 'the most' is used with:

  most adjectives with two or more syllables (e.g. modern, populated)

  Note that there are a few exceptions to the two-syllable rule.

  For example: quiet (quieter / the quietest), clever (cleverer / the cleverest)

Answers:

- good, better, the best
- bad, worse, the worst
- far, farther/further, the farthest / the furthest. *Note that two spelling variants are possible.*

Practice

Exercise 1

Do this exercise with the whole class, eliciting the correct answers. Refer students back to the rules in the Analysis section if necessary.

Answers:

1 wettest
2 best
3 further/farther
4 sunnier
5 more difficult
6 easiest
7 most beautiful
8 worst

Exercise 2

Students work in pairs and focus on accuracy. They correct grammatical and spelling mistakes in the six sentences then check with the whole class and elicit the spelling rules used here. (See below for rules.)

Answers:

1 better *(spelling)*
2 easier *(spelling)*
3 more comfortable *(grammar)* / much more complicated, *(grammar)*
4 worse *(grammar)*
5 one of the most *(grammar + missing words)*
6 hotter, than *(spelling)*

Highlight the difference in pronunciation and meaning of 'then' and 'than'.

Then – later, after that (pronunciation: /ðen/)

Than – a preposition used with comparative forms (pronunciation: /ðən/)

Rules:

1 Doubling consonants: most one-syllable adjectives that end in 'consonant + vowel + consonant' (e.g. *big*) double their last consonant (e.g. bigger, biggest).

2 '-*y*' into '-*i*': if a two-syllable adjective ends in '-*y*' and the preceding letter is a consonant, then the '-*y*' becomes an '-*i*'. (e.g. *heavy – heavier/heaviest*).

Exercise 3

In pairs students look at the seven pictures and information, and discuss the differences with their partner. Using both the comparative and superlative forms and *much/a bit* where possible, students make as many sentences as they can. Do one sentence as an example with the whole class. Encourage the use of 'a bit' and 'much'. Students write their answers on big pieces of paper. When they have finished, they should put their answers up on the walls. Each pair looks at somebody else's sentences and corrects any mistakes. Check answers with the whole class. Students write sentences for the other sections for homework.

Activate your English

Students work in small groups and discuss the topics in the table. Students compare the nouns, using the adjectives. Give students a time limit.

This activity could be done as a 'pyramid' discussion. Each group discusses the same topic (e.g. learning English). When students finish discussing the first topic, one student from each group moves to a different group. The same discussion takes place, but this time students say what the original group thought and try to justify their answers. Do the same for the other two topics of 'food' and 'jobs'.

During the discussions encourage students to justify their answers and to use comparative and superlative forms of the adjectives given.

	Country 1	**Country 2**	**Country 3**	**Country 4**
Name				
Size				
Population				
Density of population				
What mountains there are				
Average rainfall				
The average highest temperature				
The average lowest temperature				

Extra idea

Countries

Students are given a name of a country. Try to choose countries that have some superlatives about them (e.g. the smallest, the largest, the hottest, the coldest, etc.). Students work in small groups. Each group works on a different country. The research could be done for homework or in class time, if computers are available. In the following lesson, students compare their findings and prepare their presentation.

Each group gives their presentation. Other groups listen and fill in the table below with the necessary information. You will need a photocopy of the table for each student. When all the groups have finished their presentations, each group looks at the information they have put together. Students stay in the same groups and discuss the differences between the four countries, using the comparative and superlative forms.

Extra activity

Worksheet 1

Superlatives – the Earth's records

Students work in two groups (A and B) and prepare a quiz for the other group, or for another class. First, they fill in the correct superlative forms for the adjectives on the worksheet. Students are free to add whatever category they wish (there are four extra blank spaces for their own questions).

Answers:

Group A

1 the most venomous
2 the highest
3 the longest
4 the most polluted
5 the richest
6 the deepest

Group B

1 the tallest
2 the heaviest
3 the highest
4 the oldest
5 the most densely populated
6 the fastest

Students then research the information for homework and prepare multiple-choice answers (A, B or C) in class (i.e. one correct answer and two distracters). They read out the questions and the options. A point is awarded for each correct answer. Each team must have the same number of questions. The team with most points wins.

Listening

Pre-listening activity

Students work in pairs and tell each other about their different trips or holiday experiences before listening to the recording. Elicit answers from a few students.

Listening: activity 1

Students listen to six speakers and decide what kind of experience they're describing. *See Transcript 5 at the back of the Coursebook.*

Answers:

(*Allow paraphrasing*)

1 Seeing the film *Gorillas in the Mist* with her father.
2 Swimming in icy cold water.
3 Watching whales.
4 Climbing in the Himalayas.
5 Scuba diving.
6 Driving across Death Valley in California.

Listening: activity 2

Before doing activity 2, draw students' attention to the Study tip box about listening and matching speakers. Ask a few questions to check students' understanding of the type of task this is. Then students read the statements. Explain any unfamiliar vocabulary. Students listen and match the speakers to the statements. When checking answers with the whole class, ask students if they can remember what made them choose each answer.

For homework, students can read Transcript 5 and underline the answers.

Answers:

Speaker 1: G *(since that moment I've always wanted to…)*
Speaker 2: E *(sadly)*
Speaker 3: D *(I'm already planning another journey)*
Speaker 4: A *(it got a bit lonely at times / you can't really talk to anybody)*
Speaker 5: F *(I decided to apply for a job over there / I'm planning to settle down there)*
Speaker 6: B *(I never realised was how cold it gets at night / I didn't bring any warm clothes)*

Vocabulary 3

Students use an English dictionary and match the words to their correct definition. Then drill the pronunciation. Don't forget to mark the syllable stress when practising the pronunciation.

Answers:

Note that the stressed syllables are underlined.

- **A** *extinction (we always stress the syllable before -tion/-sion)*
- **B** *circulation*
- **C** *polluted*
- **D** *a hunter*
- **E** *marine*
- **F** *immune system*
- **G** *boost (one-syllable word – the whole word is stressed)*

Speaking

Ask students to look at the topics A–E. They should also look at the four guiding bullet points which will help them to develop their ideas. Students should spend a few minutes thinking about what they want to say. Draw students' attention to the useful language phrases in the Coursebook, and encourage the use of these phrases in their conversations. Students work in pairs and develop their conversations by asking additional questions about what has been said.

Extra idea

When doing pair work conversations, try to swap students round so that they speak to a different student each time they start a new conversation. In this speaking activity, students can work with a different partner each time they start a new topic A–E.

After the conversations, ask students to complete the phrases 1–8. Elicit the correct form(s) to be used in each phrase.

For homework, students choose one of the topics A–E and write a short paragraph about their experience using some of the phrases 1–8.

Tenses and verb forms:

1. When I was little, I … *(past simple, used to, would)*
2. I've always wanted to … *(infinitive form)*
3. I've always been fascinated by … *(-ing form)*
4. It wasn't until … *(e.g. last year) that I managed to … (infinitive form)*
5. In my life I've … *(past participle form) a lot of … (noun or -ing form)*
6. You might think I'm crazy, but I … *(present perfect, present simple, present continuous, going to)*
7. What I never realised was that/how … *(past simple, present tenses)*
8. I've read a lot about … *(noun or -ing form)*

Extra activity

Worksheet 2

Adjectives and syllable stress

Activity 1

Students work in pairs, look at the table and fill in the adjective forms. Write the adjectives on the board and highlight the suffix in each adjective.

Activity 2

Introduce the stress patterns in the table. Students should now use an English dictionary to look up the stress for each adjective from activity 1. Make sure that students know how stress is marked in dictionaries (the big dot represents the syllable that is stressed; the number of dots altogether is the number of syllables). Ask students to come to the board to write the correct answers under the correct stress pattern. Drill the syllable stress of the adjectives. Students can then test each other in pairs. Student A points to an adjective; student B pronounces it.

Activity 3

Students work individually and complete the questions with an adjective of their choice. Students then mingle and ask each other their questions. As feedback, ask what students found out about other students. For example, 'What did you find out about Pjotr?' Students who talked to him will tell the class.

Answers:

Activity 1

delighted/delightful

independent

fascinated/fascinating

angry

embarrassed/embarrassing

unhappy

understanding/understandable

tired/tiring

energetic/energising

fashionable

freezing/frozen

homesick (no suffix)

Activity 2

nervous
angry
tired
tiring
freezing
frozen
homesick

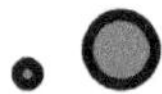 

supportive
delighted/delightful
embarrassed (Note that 'embarrassing' doesn't fit any of the syllable stress patterns in the table.)

fascinated/fascinating
educated

independent
understanding (Note that 'understandable' doesn't fit any of the syllable stress patterns in the table.)
energetic

Writing

Writing: activity 1

Students work in pairs, read the practice exam question and answer the questions. Then check answers with the whole class.

In your feedback focus on:

- Topic/contents/organisation/paragraphs
- Audience/style/register
- Word limit

Writing: activity 2

Students read the sample answer and underline the writer's views on the topic. Then they work in pairs, compare their answers and say whether they agree or disagree. Check answers with the whole class. Encourage discussion and paraphrasing of the ideas from the text.

Answers:

Writer's views on the topic

1. *Young people need to travel … it teaches you to be independent, responsible for your own actions and more organised …*
2. *Getting information from the Internet and experiencing it are two completely different things … Which experience is going to stay with you longer?*
3. *However, if you have visited a place and you felt very strongly about what you saw or learnt, this experience might help you in deciding what you want to do later in life.*

Writing: activity 3

Students read the sample answer again and analyse it in more detail. They answer questions individually, then check in pairs. Check answers with the whole class.

Answers:

1. Neutral – the public.
2. Five.
3. General introduction outlining the topic.
4. You talk to them – rhetorical questions; include examples and use a wide range of interesting and descriptive language, e.g. *immense pressure.*
5. Your views with examples and justification.
6. The conclusion, the summary of what you believe, linked back to the statement in the question.
7. Opening paragraph – what the general opinion is; paras 2–4 – linkers to introduce new ideas; closing paragraph – *overall* + personal opinion phrase.
8. 'first of all' and 'secondly' to sequence ideas; 'additionally' to show there's another similar idea; 'overall' to summarise all the previous ideas, to reinforce the overall view.
9. 'nevertheless', 'however' – contradiction; 'for example' – giving an example to support your opinion; 'also' – adding more ideas.
10. I feel that, I really believe, I do not think, I strongly believe.

Vocabulary 4

Students read the sample answer and find the words that have similar meaning. This could be done for homework.

Answers:

1. grow(ing) up
2. recently

3 widely available
4 at your fingertips
5 tag along
6 I am a big fan of
7 breathtaking
8 immense

Writing: activity 4

This activity could be done for homework. However, it is a good idea to do the planning stage in class. Students work in small groups and discuss the organisation and the content. If students struggle with ideas, help them with some suggestions.

Writing: activity 5

Students read answers written by other students. First they check the content and say if they have the same view or not.

Then they read the answer again and assess it against the checklist. Students give each other feedback. After you have corrected students' written work, encourage students to rewrite the first draft and correct their mistakes.

Summary page

Can you remember …

Answers:

- in what country the coldest inhabited place on Earth is? *(Russia)*
- **three** interesting facts about the Dead Sea? *(See the last paragraph in the Reading section and the Did you know? box for answers.)*
- which word or phrase is the odd one out: *a peak, a mount, below sea level, altitude?* Why? *(below sea level; it refers to how low a place is)*
- what these four words mean: *a sphere, the equator, a hemisphere, salinity? (See Vocabulary 1 section.)*
- what the comparative and superlative forms are for these adjectives: *good, heavy, difficult, far? (better / the best, heavier / the heaviest, more difficult / the most difficult, farther/farthest or further/furthest)*
- what the mistake is in the following sentence? *'My bag is much more new than yours.' (much newer)*
- how to use comparative adjectives correctly? Can you write **three** sentences comparing yourself and your friend? Use 'a bit' and 'much' in your sentences.
- who/what inspired one of the speakers in the listening section? *(seeing the film* Gorillas in the Mist */ Dian Fossey)*
- the **two** adjectives, from the listening vocabulary section, that are used when a) air or water becomes dirty, and b) talking about things connected with the sea? *(polluted and marine)*
- **two** linkers that mean 'and' and **two** linkers that mean 'but'? *(also/additionally, nevertheless/however)*
- one phrase that means 'I think'? *(I feel / I strongly believe)*
- how to list ideas for and against? Describe **two** advantages and **two** disadvantages of travelling on your own. Use the correct linkers to introduce your ideas. *(See the sample text in the writing section for examples on usage.)*
- how to keep readers interested when writing an article? *(rhetorical questions, giving examples, descriptive words)*

Progress check

After completing the Summary page questions, encourage students to go back to the Objectives at the beginning of the chapter and assess their learning progress. Students should use the symbols suggested in the Progress check box. This can be followed up in tutorial time with individual students.

Chapter 3 – Worksheet 1

Superlatives – the Earth's records

Group A

Questions: What's ...	A	B	C
1 (venomous) .... animal in the world?			
2 the country with (high) .... life expectancy for women?			
3 the third (long) .... river in the world?			
4 (polluted) .... city in the world?			
5 (rich) .... country in the world?			
6 (deep) .... lake in the world?			
7			
8			
9			
10			

Group B

Questions: What's ... / Who's ... (questions 1 and 4)	A	B	C
1 (tall) .... man in the world?			
2 (heavy) .... metal?			
3 (high) .... mountain in North America?			
4 (old) .... living person?			
5 (densely populated) .... country in the world?			
6 (fast) .... animal in the world?			
7			
8			
9			
10			

Chapter 3 – Worksheet 2

Adjectives and syllable stress

Activity 1

Can you complete the adjective column with the correct forms? What are the suffixes in these adjectives?

Noun	Adjective	Verb
		delight
independence		
		fascinate
anger		
		embarrass
unhappiness		
		understand
		tire
energy		
fashion		
		freeze
homesickness		

Activity 2

Look at these adjectives and put them under the correct stress pattern:
supportive / disappointed / isolated / nervous
Now do the same with the adjectives from activity 1.

O •	• O •	O • • •	• • O •

Activity 3

Can you complete the following questions with one of the adjectives from activity 2? Some questions will need more than just an adjective. Then ask other students the questions and have a conversation.

When did you last feel .... ?
When do you feel .... ?
What makes you feel .... ?
Do you think .... these days is/are .... ?
Do you think you are .... ?
What do you do when you're feeling .... ?

Chapter 4
The life of an astronaut

Reading

Pre-reading activity

Students discuss the questions in small groups. They try to predict what difficulties astronauts may face in the four mentioned areas. Use the photo to generate some ideas for the discussion.

Compare ideas with the whole class.

Reading: activity 1

Students read the text and find the relevant information. They confirm their predictions and discuss what is surprising or strange.

Reading: activity 2

Before doing this activity, check that students can remember how to guess the meaning of unknown words from the context. If necessary, direct them to the Study tip box in Chapter 2. Ask students to look at the words in the text highlighted in blue. They work in pairs and try to guess the meaning. Encourage them to look for clues in the text. For example, the word 'dehydrated' is followed by a phrase 'water has to be added to them'.

Alternatively, divide the class into two groups. Each group can guess half of the words from the text. Then pair up students so that each pair has different words. Students share their ideas. Check with the whole class. Ask students how they arrived at their guesses. Don't give the students the exact meaning of the words at this stage.

Vocabulary 1

Students work in pairs and match the definitions to the correct words in the text.

Answers:

A to be allocated for
B to expand
C dehydrated
D be tethered to
E to rinse
F crumbs
G to float
H to sip

Reading: activity 3

Students read the text and answer the questions. Remind them how to locate information quickly in a text with headings. Students then compare their answers in pairs before checking with the whole class.

Answers:

1 Routine maintenance / scientific experiments.
2 Six hours.
3 The constant noise AND the light.
4 It doesn't produce any foam / no need for any rinsing.
5 *Any two answers*: liquid foods / soup / bread.
6 Food in microgravity starts to taste bland / astronauts' taste buds become less sensitive.
7 *Allow any reasonable paraphrasing. Any two answers*: astronauts use their muscles less when in space / because the muscles weaken when in space/ weightlessness affects astronauts' bone density / so that astronauts are prepared for when they return home.

Speaking

Students work in small groups and have a discussion. One student from each group can then move to a new group and report their original group's opinions which are then discussed with the new group.

Did you know?

For homework, students can look up more interesting facts about space and the life of astronauts and add them to the Did you know? box. Students then share this information together. Students can also research the facts mentioned in the Did you know? box in more detail. For example, why can astronauts become taller in space?

Project

Give students a few minutes to prepare their answers. They think of five items which they would take to space because they are important in their life and why they would take them. Then, they discuss their selection in groups. Students report back to the whole class and say which item was the most popular among the group and why.

The second stage is a survey best done over a longer period of time. This can be done in the same class or students interview their peers from other classes. The group compiles answers and prepares the top ten (or so) selection. Feed back to the class about each group's findings.

Have a follow-on discussion about the future legacy of the students' generation.

After the discussion, ask students to write a report on things that are important for young people in their everyday life. Encourage students to use the information from their survey. Before students write their reports, elicit why we write reports, who is likely to read them and what style and register is necessary. Students discuss in groups how they would organise their ideas and how many paragraphs they would use. Set the writing of the report for homework.

Features of reports:

Reports are written for someone in charge (for example, a manager or supervisor at work) and need to be written in a formal register. Reports use headings, subheadings and bullet points to make it easier for the reader to locate the main information easily. The first paragraph introduces the aim of the report and how the information was collected. The middle paragraphs provide objective facts. The last paragraph contains personal suggestions or recommendations.

Vocabulary 2

Compound nouns

Exercise 1

Draw students' attention to the Key term box about compound nouns and then ask them to highlight some compound nouns in the text. Students identify some examples written as two words and some written as one word. For example, *sleeping bag, earplugs*, etc.

Exercise 2

Students first look at the column on the left. Students work in pairs and match the correct halves. Play the recording to check the answers. Check with students which compounds are always written as two words (*drinking water, space shuttle*). After checking, elicit further examples, from students' own experience, of compound nouns beginning with the same first halves as in the exercise. *See Transcript 6 at the back of the Coursebook.*

Answers:

1 white*board*
2 wheel*chair*
3 drinking *water*
4 rain*fall*
5 space *shuttle*
6 Face*book*
7 basket*ball*
8 bank*notes*
9 chop*sticks*
10 dead*line*
11 gold*fish*
12 key*board*
13 pick*pocket*
14 sky*scraper*
15 sun*shine*

Exercise 3 – pronunciation

Draw students' attention to the Key term boxes about syllables and syllable stress. Play the pronunciation recording again for students to listen and mark the stress. Demonstrate one or two examples with the whole class. Check answers with the whole class. Elicit the pronunciation rules from students. Play the recording again and drill the pronunciation chorally and individually.

Answers:

Where is the syllable stress in compound nouns? *The syllable stress is always on one of the syllables of the first word in the compound noun. For example: sun*shine, *drink*ing water.

Activate your English

Students work in pairs and complete the gaps. Nominate a few students to write their answers on the board. Check with the whole class. Then students work in small groups and have a discussion.

Answers:

1 goldfish
2 keyboards
3 Facebook

4 wheelchair
5 banknotes
6 deadlines
7 pickpockets
8 drinking water
9 skyscrapers
10 whiteboards

Vocabulary 3

Prefixes

Exercise 1

Read the Key term box about prefixes. There are two types of prefixes (i.e. those that create the opposite meaning to the original word and those that create a new meaning).

Students scan the reading text and find four examples of prefixes.

Answers:

- The four words with prefixes in the reading text are *impossible, international, dehydrated* and *bicycle*.
- The word which has a prefix that makes the word negative is *impossible*.
- The words which have a prefix that adds new meaning are *international, dehydrated* and *bicycle*.
- The meaning of these prefixes are: '*inter*' – together, between, among / '*de*' – separation / '*bi*' – two.

Exercise 2

Divide the class into three groups (or six if the class is too big). Each group focuses on one prefix. Dictate the following words to students. Each group only writes down the words that can be used with their prefix. Then students show their answers to the whole class and check that everyone has written the correct answers.

Words for dictation:

- historic
- lingual
- forestation
- frost
- annual
- paid
- monthly
- prepared
- activate

Answers:

bi
- lingual
- annual
- monthly

pre
- historic
- paid
- prepared

de
- forestation
- frost
- activate

Exercises 3 and 4

Students look at some more prefixes in pairs and decide which prefix is needed for each column of words. Then, in Exercise 4, students match the prefixes to the correct meaning. The meaning includes the prefixes in Exercises 2 and 3. Students identify which prefixes are commonly used with a hyphen.

Answers:

Exercise 3

A post
B self-
C over
D under
E non-
F anti

non-, self- often need a hyphen

Exercise 4

1 over
2 under
3 self
4 post
5 pre
6 bi
7 de
8 anti
9 non

Exercise 5 – pronunciation

Students listen to a few words with prefixes. Before you play the recording, (see Transcript 7) explain the stress patterns. Explain to students that the big dot means the syllable that is stressed. The number of dots altogether is the number of syllables. Students listen, decide where the stress is and write the word in the correct column. They check in pairs. Play the recording again and check with the whole class. Drill chorally and individually. Ask students to practise saying the words correctly in pairs. Elicit from students whether the prefix is the stressed syllable in the word.

Answer:

The prefix is rarely the stressed part of the word.
ooO - oversleep, overeat, underpaid
oOo - self-service, non-smoking
oOoo - postgraduate, self-discipline, self-confident
ooOo - non-judgemental, postproduction, anti-social

Extra idea
Cut two sets of small cards. Write the words from the recording on one set of cards. Copy the stress patterns onto another set of cards. Give one card to each student (cards with words can be repeated in a large class). The students with stress pattern cards hum the stress pattern and walk round the room listening for the correct words for their group. Students with word cards walk round repeating the word. They have to try and find the correct stress pattern to match their word. Make sure this is a listening, not a reading, exercise. Students should not show their cards, but pronounce what is on the card.

When all the groups are formed, play the recording and students check that they are in the right group, holding their word up for other students to see. Play the recording again and drill the pronunciation.

Activate your English

Students work in pairs and rewrite a part of each sentence with the most suitable word/phrase containing a prefix. Do one as an example with the whole class. The words required for answers are taken from Exercises 2 and 3.

Students discuss the questions in small groups.

Answers:

1 Do you think it's important to *be bilingual* these days? Why? Why not?

2 What do you know about the issue of *deforestation* in order to use the land in other ways? Can you think of examples of how this affects the area and the living things there?

3 How popular is *pre-prepared* supermarket food in your country? How healthy do you think it is?

4 In what jobs are people *underpaid*, or *overpaid*? Can you give some examples and explain why you think that?

5 Are there problems with *antisocial behaviour* in your country? How do you think these people should be punished?

6 Do you agree with the idea that all public places should be *non-smoking*? What benefits does it bring?

7 In your opinion, do astronauts need a lot of *self-discipline*? Why?

8 Have you ever *overslept*? When? What happened next?

Extra idea
If the classroom layout allows, ask students to stand in two circles. One circle faces outwards and the other inwards. Every student from the outer circle has to be facing one student from the inner circle. Read out a statement/question; students discuss this with their partner. Each time you read out a new statement/question, the outer circle has to move clockwise so that each time they speak with a different classmate. If there is an odd number of students, the odd student can join whatever pair they want and have a three-way discussion.

Extra activity

Worksheet 1

Prefixes and compounds dominoes

This game is good to consolidate any vocabulary where two parts need to be matched together.

Cut up the blank domino cards as indicated on the worksheet. Students work in pairs. Each pair should get one whole set of blank cards. Each pair then prepares the domino cards by filling out the boxes with the required vocabulary items.

Ask students to think of various compound nouns. Each blank card has two boxes. Students should write the first part of the compound in the right-hand box of one card, and the second part in the left-hand box on a new card. Continue until all the domino cards are used. The same should be done with words with prefixes. While the prefix is written in the right-hand box on one card, the root of the word should be written in the left-hand box on another card. Ask students to put the cards in a line as they write them. The last pair of words should be on the right-hand side of the last card and on the left-hand side of the first card. This will eliminate problems later on when other students try to put the words together into a circle or a square.

When students have finished preparing the cards, they should mix them up and swap them with the pair next to them. Each pair should then put their cards in the right order to make a circle. The first pair to complete this game correctly wins.

This game can be played in the same way to practise words with prefixes.

Listening

Pre-listening activity

Ask students if they know any famous astronauts. Students work in small groups and discuss what they know about famous astronauts.

Listening: activity 1

Students listen to the first part of a talk on the radio given by an astronaut. Ask them to listen for any personal details and try to remember them. Play the recording up to '*... pursue my real ambition to become an astronaut.*' Students compare the details in pairs.

Listening: activity 2

First check with students that they can remember how to answer this exam-type question. Draw their attention to the Listening section in Chapter 2 to remind them.

Students look through the gapped profile and predict the missing information. Play the whole recording twice (Transcript 8). Students fill in the missing information. They compare their answers in pairs then with the whole class.

Answers:

a the United States / the USA
b waiter
c 1961
d 50 OR fifty
e restricted diet
f shoes
g friendly
h research scientist

Speaking

In small groups students discuss the three points. Each group selects a 'spokesperson' to report back to the whole class.

Language focus

Modal verbs and other phrases of obligation

Analysis

First draw students' attention to the Key term box and make sure students understand what 'obligation' is. Students work in small groups and work through the grammar analysis questions. Then, they compare their answers with the group next to them and discuss the grammar point. Check answers with the whole class.

Answers:

A have to / must / are required to / are obliged to
Note that 'need to' is also possible here. However, this verb doesn't appear in Transcript 8.
B should
C can
D mustn't/can't

Modal verbs and phrases without 'to':

must/should/mustn't/can

Modal verbs and phrases with 'to':

have to / are obliged to / are required to

Go through the sentences in 1–5 with the whole class. Students decide if the underlined modal verbs have the same meaning and also answer the questions about their meaning. You may have to add extra concept-checking questions where necessary. Try to use the same phrases as in the Analysis part, A–D, to ensure consistency (e.g. *it is necessary*, etc.)

Answers:

1 **A** Can't' and 'mustn't' have the same meaning.
B You can be 5 minutes late.
2 **A** These have the same meaning.
B In both sentences.
3 **A** These have the same meaning.
B In both sentences.

4 **A** The sentences have different meanings.

B In our school you have to wear a uniform at school; you get into trouble if you don't.

C In some countries you don't have to wear a uniform at school. (*lack of obligation*)

Highlight the difference between: 'have to' and 'don't have to' / 'must' and 'mustn't'.

5 **A** Slightly different meaning.

B You must see the doctor; this could be something more serious.

Practice

Exercise 1

Students do this exercise in pairs. Then check with the whole class.

Answers:

1 have to / are obliged to / are required to / must
2 can
3 have to / are obliged to / are required to / must
4 can't / mustn't / shouldn't
5 can't / mustn't
6 don't have to
7 have to / are obliged to / are required to / must
8 can't / mustn't
9 have to / are obliged to / are required to / must
10 should / must

Exercise 2

Students work in small groups and put together ten school rules they think are important. Monitor students' work and encourage the use of a wider range of structures. Also, encourage the correct use of capital letters and punctuation.

Feed back as a class. Students explain their choices and discuss the rules. For homework, students choose a public place and write some rules for it. Students read out their rules at the start of the following lesson. Other students guess the place.

Activate your English

Students work in small groups and discuss together the selection of jobs and the obligation, or lack of it, each job involves. Then have a whole class discussion.

Extra idea

Students write a short paragraph about what they expect from a job (e.g. *I want to work during the day, I want to work with a lot of people, I don't like working indoors*). Redistribute these descriptions among students. They read the paragraph and suggest a job. Students explain why they think this job would be good for that particular student. For example, 'You should be a teacher because you're not obliged to work at the weekend' OR 'You should be a zookeeper because you don't have to sit in an office all day long.'

Reading and writing

Reading: activity 1

Students read the first two paragraphs and focus on Alessio's personal details. Then, they work in pairs and write down as many details as they can remember. Tell students that they need to look for these kinds of details, and also other information, when filling in a form (see Study tip).

Reading: activity 2

Before doing activity 2, draw students' attention to the Study tip box about filling a form. Ask students to read the tips individually and then ask guiding questions to check their understanding. For example, *What words may appear in the form? What do you read first, the form or the text? Why is it a good idea to underline words/ phrases in the text?* etc.

Students do activity 2 in pairs and familiarise themselves with the conventions of form-filling.

Answers:

1 B
2 E
3 D
4 A
5 C
6 F

Reading: activity 3

Students look at the form and discuss what sort of information is required. Then, they read the text about Alessio and find the information in the text and fill in the form. Encourage students to underline the answers in the text. Students compare their answers in pairs before checking with the whole class.

Answers:

Training programme for young astronauts

Section A

Full name: *Alessio Francesco Grossi*

Gender: *male*

Address: *4 Ashland Avenue, Chicago, Illinois, USA*

Date of birth: *17th September 1996 (OR 17/09/1996)*

Mobile/Cell phone number: *078 602 9937*

Email address: *alessio1@hotmail.com*

Preferred method of contact (please tick):

Phone ☐ Email ☑ By post ☐

Section B

Languages spoken: *English, Italian*

How would you describe your level of fitness (please circle):

poor average good (excellent)

Preferred length of course (please delete):

~~six months~~ / *one year*

Section C

In the space below, write one sentence giving your reason for choosing this programme, and one sentence giving details of how this program me would help you in your future studies/career.

Example sentence 1: I would like to train at the Johnson Space Center in future and my dream is to become an astronaut.

Example sentence 2: It will teach me very useful skills and give me a lot of self-discipline.

OR It will help me in all sorts of jobs and look good on my curriculum vitae.

TEACHING TIP

When preparing for this type of exam-style question, make sure your students are aware of the following:

- The correct use of capital letters throughout the form is required.
- When writing an address, do **not** include prepositions (e.g. *in Chicago*).
- Students must answer according to the rubric (see Reading: activity 2).
- When writing sentences, students must **not** start with a conjunction (e.g. *because, so, and, but*).
- Students should pay attention to accuracy of grammar, spelling, punctuation and relevance.

Extra idea

Alternatively, write these rules without *'must/mustn't'* on cards. For example, ***use capital letters in addresses, use prepositions in addresses***. Students work in groups and discuss whether these are things they should or should not do.

Do this awareness-raising activity before doing Writing: activity 5.

Writing: activity 1

Elicit from students when we need to use capital letters in English. Students circle the correct words in activity 1. Ask students to provide examples to support their ideas.

Pay attention to students' handwriting. Emphasise the need for clarity in letter formation where the capital letters are the same as their lower-case variant. For example, 'w' and 'W', 'y' and 'Y'. Encourage students to be aware of the difference between letters that extend below the line and those that sit on the line. Use dictation as an activity to practise handwriting.

Answers:

days, first names, months, school language subjects, surnames, names of cities, street names, countries, nationality, languages

Note that this is just a selection of the most common categories and that there are more instances when capital letters need to be used. Point out that pronouns do not need capital letters with the exception of *I*, which always has one.

Writing: activity 2

Read through the Key term box about punctuation. Ask students to match the punctuation marks to their correct name.

Answers:

A H

B !

C .

D It's

E ?

F ,

Writing: activity 3

Go through the activity with the whole class. Nominate students to name the marks and elicit when we use them. Project the text onto the board if possible.

Answers:

(Correct punctuation marks are shown by the underlines.)

1. What's your name? *(start of a sentence / short verb form / end of a question)*
2. I've never eaten seafood, lamb or avocado. *(I / short verb form / separating list items / end of a sentence)*
3. Peter! Wait! *(first name / exclamation / start of a sentence / exclamation)*
4. If you don't study hard, you'll fail your exam. *(start of a sentence/ short verb form / separating a clause / short verb form / end of a sentence)*
5. This is Katie's coat. She must have forgotten it. *(start of a sentence / first name / possessive apostrophe / end of a sentence)*

Note that students may find the different use of the apostrophe in *'Katie's car'* and *'Katie's happy'* confusing. Take this opportunity to highlight the difference.

Writing: activity 4

Students work in pairs and correct the mistakes in punctuation. Check with the whole class.

Alternatively: This exercise could be done for homework.

Answers:

(Incorrect punctuation marks are shown by the underlines.)

1. Ive told you many times. (1 mistake) *(I've told you many times.)*
2. Can i ask you what time it is. (2 mistakes) *(Can I ask you what time it is?)*
3. If i were you I wouldn't do it (3 mistakes) *(If I were you, I wouldn't do it.)*
4. She want's to be an astronaut. (1 mistake) *(She wants to be an astronaut.)*
5. I want to go to tokyo New york and paris. (4 mistakes) *(I want to go to Tokyo, New York and Paris.)*

Extra activity

Worksheet 2

Proofreading practice

Divide the class into two groups – group A and group B. Each group has a copy of the relevant section of Worksheet 2 (A or B). Students look at the sentences and correct the punctuation errors by working together in their groups. Then students work in pairs – student A and student B. This part of the exercise is to focus on dictation.

Student A reads out the sentences (including the label A–F) in their section of the worksheet. Student B writes down the missing sentences on the lines provided. If student B is correct, the sentences should be identical to student A's sentences. The same is done with student B's sentences. Check answers with the whole class.

Answers:

A I read Peter's email about his new course. It sounds really interesting.

B Mary's moved to a new house. She lives at 78 Green Street now.

C It's such a nice day today. What are you doing this afternoon?

D I've been to India many times. When I went there last time, it was extremely hot.

E Who's that girl talking to Jessica? Do you know her?

F The new principal decided to change the school's name to the New Zealand Academy.

Writing: activity 5

Look at the Extra idea at the top of the previous page. Writing: activity 1. It is a good idea to do this activity before doing activity 5.

Divide the class into four groups. Students analyse the errors and rewrite the answers correctly. Check answers with the whole class.

Answers:

1. *Punctuation errors / poor grammar.*

   I like Oxford. I studied English in China for two years.
2. *Spelling errors / there are four sentences instead of two.*

   Possible answer: I heard that Oxford is a beautiful city and there are very good language schools. I've been studying English for four years now and want to continue my studies in the UK to improve my pronunciation.
3. *Punctuation errors / should be written in the first person, not the third person*

   I want to study in Oxford because my sister lives there and I want to be near her. I studied English at primary school a long time ago, but only for three years.
4. *The first sentence starts with 'because' / errors in capital letters.*

   My friend was there and liked it very much. I've been studying English by myself on the Internet and by watching American films.

Writing: activity 6

This activity can be done for homework. In the following lesson ask students to swap their answers and check for spelling/grammatical/punctuation errors. Encourage peer correction.

Alternatively:

This activity can be done as a group exercise. Divide the class into six groups. Two groups work on the same question. Then, they swap their answers, compare and check for errors.

Summary page

Extra idea

This revision page can be done as a competition. Divide the class into groups. Don't let students see the questions. Enlarge and photocopy the questions. Then cut up the questions into sets; one set per group. Students work through the questions, but have to show the teacher the answer each time. They aren't allowed to answer the following question until they get the first one right and so on. The winner is the team with no question strips left. Check answers with the whole class.

Can you remember …

Answers:

- how astronauts sleep? (*See Reading section; paragraph about sleeping.)*
- which verb is connected with movement: *to expand, to float, to sip?(to float)*
- which word(s) are connected with water: *crumbs, dehydrated, to rinse, to sip? (dehydrated, to rinse, to sip)*
- what a compound noun is? *(two words that make up a new word)*
- how to make a compound noun with 'rain', 'gold' and 'bank'? *(rainfall, goldfish, banknote)*
- **four** prefixes, what they mean and give an example with a word for each of them? *(See 'Vocabulary' 3 section.)*
- where the syllable stress is in: *oversleep, postgraduate and self-discipline*?
- **three** words that need a hyphen? *(Words with the following prefixes often need a hyphen: self-, non-)*
- where the Johnson Space Center is? *(Houston, Texas)*
- **two** things astronauts have to do during their training? *(for example, pass a swimming test, get a scuba certificate)*

- **three** words/phrases that mean the same as 'must'? *(have to, are obliged to, are required to)*
- how to talk about rules? Make **three** sentences about rules in your school. *(students' own answers)*
- the difference in meaning between 'You mustn't come on Friday' and 'You don't have to come on Friday?' *(They have different meanings. 'Mustn't' = it is important that you don't come; 'don't have to' = it's not necessary for you to come – you have a choice.)*
- in what 'person' you should fill in a form? *(in the first person)*
- when we use capital letters in English? Give **five** examples. *(See Writing: activity 1. e.g. Kate, Paris, Monday, Maths, September.)*
- what each of these is called? ? , ' ! . (*a question mark / a comma / an apostrophe / an exclamation mark / a full stop)*
- how to use the punctuation marks from the previous question? Can you use the marks in sentences? *(students' own answers)*

Progress check

After completing the Summary page questions, encourage students to go back to the Objectives at the beginning of the chapter and assess their learning progress. Students should use the symbols suggested in the Progress check box. This can be followed up in tutorial time with individual students.

Chapter 4 – Worksheet 1
Prefixes and compounds dominoes

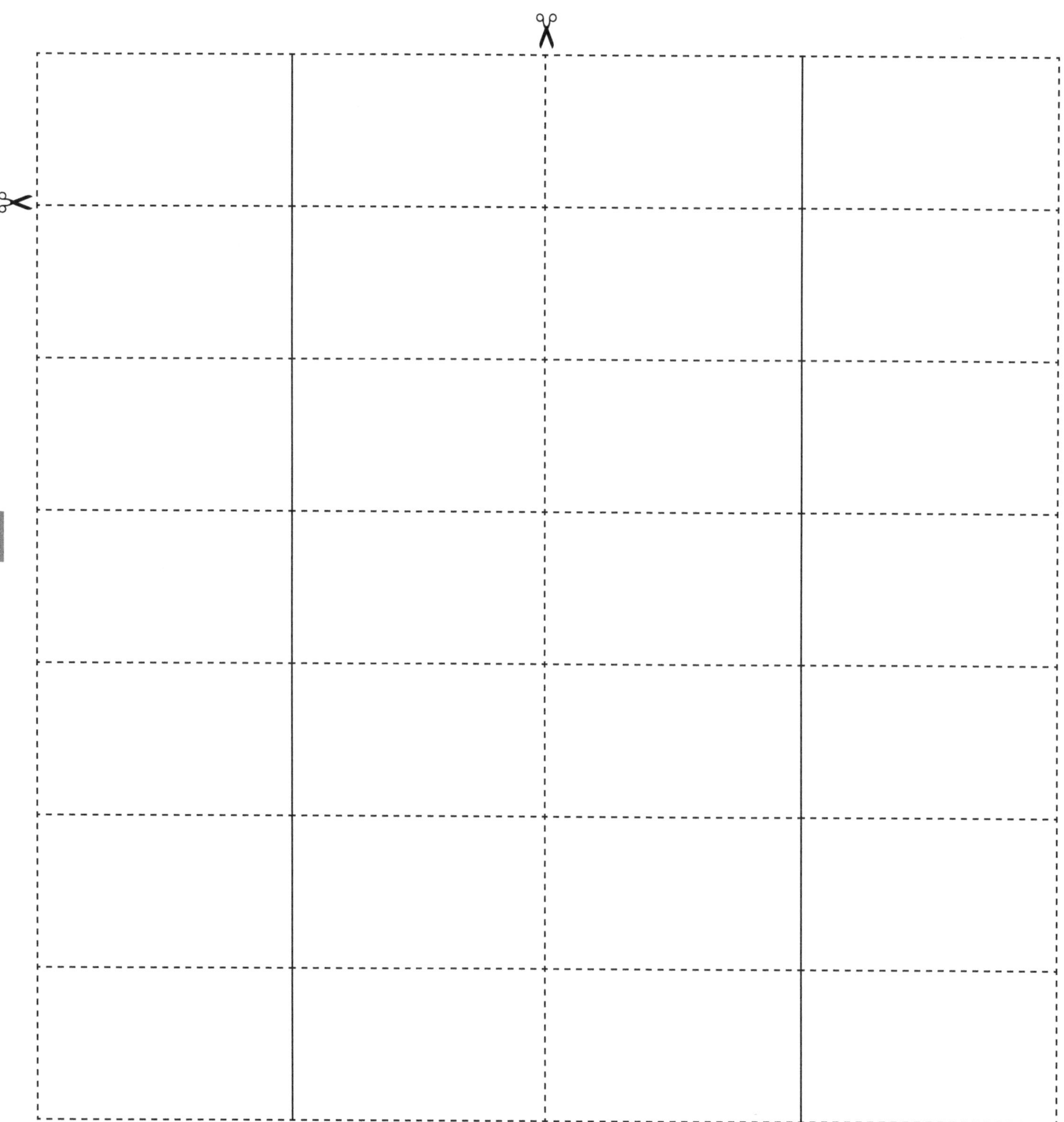

Chapter 4 – Worksheet 2
Proofreading practice

Student A

A i read peters email about his new course it sounds really interesting

B ……………………………………………………………………………

C its such a nice day today what are you doing this afternoon

D ……………………………………………………………………………

E whos that girl talking to jessica do you know her

F ……………………………………………………………………………

……………………………………………………………………………

Student B

A ……………………………………………………………………………

B marys moved to a new house she lives at 78 green street now

C ……………………………………………………………………………

D ive been to india many times when i went there last time it was extremely hot

E ……………………………………………………………………………

……………………………………………………………………………

F the new principal decided to change the schools name to the new zealand academy

Chapter 5
Social media

Reading and writing

Pre-reading activity

Students work in groups. They talk about their personal experiences with social networking. Draw their attention to the pictures and ask them to discuss the advantages and disadvantages of social networking sites. Students choose one member from their group to write down their suggestions. Then they share their ideas with the whole class.

Reading: activity 1

This activity is done as 'jigsaw reading'. Divide the class into two groups. Group A reads Article A about the advantages of social networking and group B reads Article B about the disadvantages. They read the text and underline examples of advantages and disadvantages. First they compare within each of their groups (A and B). After that students work in pairs so that student A works together with student B. They tell each other what they found out.

Note that students should be told that the underlining in paragraph one does not refer to this activity. It is needed in activity 2.

Answers:

Advantages – *stay in touch with other people; help people to find their childhood friends; renewing long-lost friendships; catch up with friends and keep up with their news on an almost daily basis; keeping up to date; a great way of finding out about upcoming job opportunities / people can promote their business; artists can inform fans about their gigs, or latest exhibitions; allow the public to give instant feedback on the artists' work; people can interact with their favourite artist; how easy it is to organise an event with your friends; people can invite the right group of friends to attend an event; friends can invite each other to participate and compete in a variety of games without leaving their homes*

Disadvantages – *how much easier it has become for your personal details to be accessed online; dishonest people target other people with endless junk mail; dishonest people can hijack other people's email accounts; attempts to access people's bank accounts / attempts to steal people's identity; scammers trick the users into downloading harmful software; scammers can access the person's friend list and try to send the malware to their friends too; it's overwhelming; it's addictive; a lot of constant updates; to keep checking; can distract people from whatever they are doing*

Vocabulary 1

Students work in the same groups and find the words in the text they read in activity 1 and circle them. They try to guess the meaning and then check in an English dictionary to confirm their guesses.

Students work in pairs A + B again and tell each other what their words mean. Check the correct meanings with the whole class.

Reading: activity 2

Tell students they are going to do a note-taking exercise. First draw students' attention to the Key term box about topic sentences and the Study tip box about note-taking. Ask students to look at the first paragraph of Article A and go through it with the whole class. Do one more paragraph with the whole class underlining the supporting ideas for the topic sentence highlighted and check that students understand the activity.

Students work in pairs and find the supporting ideas in the rest of the text. Check with the whole class. If possible, project the text onto the board.

Answers:

The main reason why most people sign up to social networking sites is to stay in touch with other people. These sites also help people to find their childhood friends that they have lost touch with. Renewing these long-lost friendships is just a click away. It is very exciting to be able to catch up with friends and keep up with their news on an almost daily basis thanks to frequent updates.

Keeping up to date, however, doesn't have to be restricted to friends and acquaintances. What many people tend to forget is that they can also use networking sites for professional reasons. It is actually a great way of finding out about upcoming job opportunities. Friends might know about job vacancies that may not be advertised elsewhere or they can even recommend their friends for certain jobs. Even people already employed can promote their business online. This is particularly important for artists, actors and musicians who can create pages devoted to their band or theatre company, and inform fans about their gigs, or latest exhibitions. In addition, the sites can be used to allow the public to give instant feedback on the artists' work and to interact with their favourite artist.

Another great plus of social networking sites is how easy it is to organise an event with your friends. Thanks to different settings people can organise their friends by different criteria. These criteria could be how close friends they are, common interests and hobbies or where they live. This means if a certain event takes place, e.g., an open-air concert or a football match, all they have to do is invite the right group of friends to attend. Some networking sites offer a range of quizzes and games, so friends living on opposite sides of the globe can invite each other to participate and compete in a variety of games without leaving their homes.

Reading: activity 3

Students read Article A and complete the notes. They check in pairs before checking with the whole class.

Answers:

The most common reasons given for joining social networking sites *(any three from the list)*

- find childhood friends
- renew long-lost friendships
- catch up with friends
- keep up with friends' news on an almost daily basis

How social networking sites can help people to look for work *(any two from the list)*

- find out about upcoming job opportunities
- friends might know about job vacancies
- friends can recommend their friends for certain jobs

What types of outdoor social activities can be arranged online

- an open-air concert
- a football match

> **TEACHING TIP**
> Please note that in a note-taking exercise, there is no need for students to paraphrase the information they find in the text. However, answers should be brief and concise.

Reading: activity 4

Students revise the steps they should take when doing this kind of exercise, i.e.

- Read the question and the rubrics very carefully.
- Locate the correct paragraph by finding the topic sentences necessary for each rubric.
- Underline examples supporting the topic sentence.
- Write brief answers under the correct heading.

This activity could be set for homework or done under exam conditions in class time. Students do this reading activity on their own.

Answers:

The dangers of revealing too much personal information online *(any three from the list)*

- dishonest people can target other people with endless junk mail
- dishonest people can hijack other people's email
- dishonest people can access people's bank accounts
- dishonest people can steal other people's identity

What damage scammers can do

- trick people into downloading malware / trick people into downloading a virus
- scammers access the person's friend list and send malware to people's friends

Consequences of constant updates *(any two from the list)*

- difficult to find specific information
- tempting to keep checking
- distract people from whatever they are doing

Writing: activity 1

Draw students' attention to the Key term and Study tip boxes about writing a summary.

Students read the task in activity 1. Analyse the task with the whole class. Then students look at the sample answer and answer the questions about this text in pairs.

Answers:

1. Social networking sites have many advantages.
2. No. It's only one sentence due to the word limit restriction. The main focus should be on the examples of advantages.

3 Social networking sites have many advantages. These sites give us the opportunity to rediscover friends we thought we had lost. We can follow what our existing friends do every day. People can look for a job on these sites. Our friends might know what jobs are going to become available. They can suggest us for jobs to other people. If you want to go out with your friends, it is easier to invite them.

4 For example, *rediscover* – find friends they have lost touch with; *every day* – on a daily basis; *suggest us for jobs* – recommend friends for certain jobs, etc.

5 There are no linkers to connect ideas within the sentence, or within the paragraph.

TEACHING TIP

Encourage students to link ideas in a logical order and paraphrase the idea they extract from the main text. Also focus on grammatical accuracy and appropriate vocabulary.

Students should be encouraged to use their own words and to write accurately (spelling, grammar, punctuation). They should also pay attention to the relevance of the content they write.

Writing: activity 2

Students insert the three linkers into the sample summary. Do this with the whole class. If possible, project the text onto the board. Highlight the use of a comma with these linkers.

Answers:

Social networking sites have many advantages. **First of all,** these sites give us the opportunity to rediscover friends we thought we had lost. We can follow what our existing friends do every day. **Moreover,** people can look for a job on these sites. Our friends might know what jobs are going to become available. They can suggest us for jobs to other people. **Finally**, if you want to go out with your friends, it is easier to invite them.

(79 words)

Writing: activity 3

Students work in pairs and match the linkers to those in activity 2.

Answers:

- First of all: to begin with / firstly
- Moreover: furthermore / what is more / also *(Note that* also *can be used at the start of a sentence or between the first two verbs.)*
- Finally: last but not least

Writing and speaking: activity 4

Students work in groups of three. Each student chooses one of the topics and spends a few minutes preparing what to say. Encourage students to prepare notes about what they want to say. Students then give a short talk, using the linkers from activities 2 and 3. Students should make four points. Nominate three students (one for each topic) to give their talk to the class. This can be followed up by a class discussion.

Writing: activity 5

Students read the question. They plan the summary in pairs before writing it. They should think of ideas they want to include and in what order. Students then write their summary. This could be done for homework.

Writing: activity 6

Draw students' attention to the checklist in the Coursebook. Ask them to exchange their summaries and compare the ideas included by their partner. Then students read the summary again and check it against the checklist.

Vocabulary 2

Students work in three groups. As a reminder, refer students to the Key term box about Vocabulary sets in Chapter 3 (page 33 in the Coursebook). Each group focuses on one vocabulary set in Article B. Students can refer back to Chapter 3 to see what word families are and why they are useful for them.

Students scan the text and find as many words connected with the word family as they can. The first one has been done as an example. Note that some of the words can be used in more than one spidergram.

Check answers with the whole class.

Suggested answers:

'Computer words' with negative meaning: *junk mail, hijack an email account, scammer, malware, harmful software, a virus, be infected with a virus*

Words connected with activities you can do on the computer: *sign up to / join networking sites, click, create pages, interact, have different settings, access online, download, install a program, share information online*

Words connected with social networking sites: *stay in touch, frequent updates, organise friends by different criteria, share information, receive a link, friend list, constant updates, feeds, links, posts*

Speaking 1

Students work in small groups and discuss the questions. Encourage the use of the words from Vocabulary 2.

Project

Students are going to research how much time young people in their school spend on the computer and what they mainly use it for. They will prepare a questionnaire with the whole class. Students negotiate what questions they would like to include. Keep this questionnaire relatively short. Students work in groups and decide what age group they want to interview. This could be different ages at your school. Afterwards, students compare their findings within the group. Encourage students to prepare a graph/chart to represent their findings. Each group presents their findings to the rest of the class.

Discuss students' findings together with the class.

After the discussion, ask students to write a report to highlight their findings. Before students write their reports, elicit why we write reports, who is likely to read them and what style and register are necessary. Students discuss in groups how they would organise their ideas and how many paragraphs they would use. Set the writing of the report for homework.

Features of reports:

Reports are written for someone in charge (for example, a manager or supervisor at work) and need to be written in a formal register. Reports use headings, subheadings and bullet points to make it easier for the reader to locate the main information easily. The first paragraph introduces the aim of the report and how the information was collected. The middle paragraphs provide objective facts. The last paragraph contains personal suggestions or recommendations.

Language focus

The first conditional and other future clauses

Analysis

Students work in small groups, analyse the three sentences and answer the questions below.

Answers:

1 The future.

2 Yes, there is a real possibility for the situation to happen.

3 Two: the 'if clause' and the 'main clause'.

4 Present simple or present continuous, but the meaning is still about the future.

5 We can use 'will', 'going to', present continuous with future meaning or modal verbs. In some cases we can also use the imperative form.

6 We use the main clause to make questions. For example, the question from the conditional sentence 'If it rains, I won't go out' would be 'Will you go out if it rains?' Ask students to make questions from the three example conditional sentences.

7 No, we can start the sentence with the main clause: 'I'll stay in if the weather is bad tomorrow.'

8 Yes, but only if the sentence starts with the 'if clause': 'If the weather is bad, I'll stay in.'

Other linkers:

Do the rest of the language analysis about other future clauses with the whole class.

Explain to students that other future clauses have the same rules as the first conditional. Draw their attention to other time linkers used in future clauses. Ask students to underline the tenses and verb forms and elicit the grammatical forms.

Answers:

1 As soon as I <u>get</u> there (present simple), I'<u>ll let</u> you know I'm safe and sound. (future simple '*will*')

2 When he <u>finishes</u> his homework (present simple), he<u>'s going</u> out with his friends. (present continuous with future meaning)

3 Until you <u>tell</u> me the truth (present simple), I <u>can't help</u> you. (modal verb with future meaning)

4 Unless it<u>'s</u> very cold (present simple), we<u>'re going</u> for a walk near the lake tomorrow. (present continuous with future meaning)

5 I'<u>ll come</u> (future simple '*will*') to say goodbye before I <u>go</u> home. (present simple)

Meaning:

Students look at the pairs of sentences and explain any difference in meaning.

Answers:

A Almost the same. 'As soon as' is more urgent and means 'immediately after something happens'. 'When' is more general.

B The same.

C The same.

D 'If' is used to express a future possibility here, i.e. 'maybe I want, maybe I don't want'; 'when' is used to express a more real situation i.e. 'I want to – it's just a question of when'. For example, *When I get home, I'll have something to eat.* – This means: 'I'll definitely get home'. *If I get home, I'll have something to eat.* – This means: 'I might not get home.'

Practice

Exercise 1

Do this exercise with the whole class.

Answers:

1 doesn't rain / I'll go
2 decides / we're meeting OR we'll meet
3 have / can't finish OR won't be able to finish
4 will you do / doesn't come
5 open / should talk
6 hear OR have heard / can / tell
7 She'll be / don't come
8 might leave / gets

Exercise 2

Students complete the sentences with their own ideas. They can write these ideas up for homework.

Activate your English

Work in small groups and discuss their future plans using the incomplete sentences. Students use these sentences as opening statements for their dialogue.

Extra idea

If you feel students need more fluency practice in this area, you can use any problem-solving task to practise this language item. For example, choose six items from a selection to do an activity, such as going for a holiday, or preparing a meal for a party. Students discuss the items they want to select using the first conditional or other future clauses. For example, *If I go on my own, I'll definitely take an iPod with me. I won't take an umbrella. When I get there, I can always buy one.*

Extra activity

Worksheet 1

Future clauses

Cut up the right-hand column of the grid into 14 cards. Students work in pairs and match the correct halves. They can test each other by putting down one strip at a time. Their partner has to say the correct first half as quickly as possible. Then students look at the first halves only and complete the sentences with their own examples.

Listening

Pre-listening activity

Ask students if they know what a generation gap is and to give examples of it from their own experience.

Students look at the pictures and guess what the topic of the recording will be. They work in small groups and discuss their ideas about the impact of the Internet on the relationship between the two generations.

Listening: activity 1

Play the first part of the programme (up to '*…, which is really sad to see*'). Students listen for examples of the impact of the Internet on the two generations.

Vocabulary 3

Give each pair (or each student) one word or phrase. Students look up the meaning in an English dictionary and then explain the meaning to the whole class. Encourage paraphrasing, rather than students reading out the exact dictionary entry.

Listening: activity 2

Students look at the questions and highlight key words. Then play the whole recording. Students choose the best option for each question. Then, they check their answers in pairs before checking with the whole class. If necessary, play the recording again. Alternatively, students read Transcript 9 for homework and underline the correct answers in the text.

Answers:

1 B
2 C
3 A
4 C

5 B
6 A
7 C
8 B

Extra activity

Worksheet 2

Phrasal verbs with *up* and *out*

Cut up the cards (one set per pair or group). Students match the correct pairs together. Ask them to choose five phrasal verbs and write gapped sentences. They read out their sentences to the pair next to them. The other pair has to guess the correct phrasal verb. Students do the mingling activity 'Find somebody who …'. First students have to prepare questions. Students mingle and try to find somebody who answers 'yes' to their question. They then ask an additional question (see brackets on the worksheet for suggestions).

Writing

Writing: activity 1

Tell students that they may have to write an article in the form of a piece of discursive writing on a given topic. Ask them to read the Study tip box about writing an article. Good answers can address the topic from both sides of the argument or from one side.

Students re-read Article B, in the Reading and writing section. With the whole class, discuss whether this piece of writing looks at the topic from one side (a one-sided article) or from two sides (a balanced article).

Answer:

It is a one-sided article as it deals with the negative aspects only.

Writing: activity 2

Students work in pairs and match the highlighted words from Article B to the correct language function.

Answers:

1 One of the biggest drawbacks is …
2 Another big (online) threat is … / … also means that …
3 On the one hand, … / on the other hand, …
4 For example, …
5 it can … as well as …
6 All in all, … / outweigh the disadvantages.

Speaking 2

Students work in pairs and choose one topic from the list. They spend a few minutes preparing what they want to say. Then they talk to each other, trying to use as many linkers from Writing activity 2 as they can. Nominate a student to give their talk to the whole class. Then organise a class discussion based on the ideas from the student's talk.

Writing: activity 3

Students choose one topic from the list in the previous speaking activity and write an article. This could be the same topic as in the speaking activity or a different one. First elicit the audience and the appropriate register (audience – other students, register – semi-formal). Students write their articles in class or for homework. Encourage students to proofread their written work.

Display students' work around the room. Students read the articles and discuss the ideas mentioned in pairs.

TEACHING TIP

Remind students that their answer should not be considerably shorter than the required word length. This will be because they haven't included enough information to demonstrate sufficient understanding of the topic or of the task.

Summary page

Can you remember …

Students work in groups and answer the questions. This activity could be done as a group competition. You can either allow students to use their books to check the answers or do this activity as a memory check.

Check answers with the whole class, awarding points for each correct answer.

Answers:

- **three** advantages and **three** disadvantages of social networking sites? *(For example: Advantages – making connection with other people; easier to invite friends to an event; for artists to promote their work. Disadvantages – receiving junk mail; getting computer viruses; people constantly checking updates. For more examples, see Articles A and B in the Reading and writing section.)*

- what these three words / phrases mean: *to catch up with somebody, dilemma, overwhelming? (to meet somebody after a long time to talk about what they have been doing / a situation when a difficult decision has to be made / this adjective describes a very strong emotion or action that you find difficult to control)*
- what a topic sentence is and why it is important? *(The main sentence in a paragraph that introduces the topic of that paragraph; it is important as any other information will only give supporting information. This is important to know when locating specific ideas/ opinions in a text.)*
- **two** synonyms for 'moreover' and one synonym for 'finally'? Can you make sentences with these? *(furthermore / also / last but not least)*
- **two** words connected with computer activities? *(See Vocabulary 2 in the Teacher's Book for answers.)*
- what is wrong with the following sentences? 'If he go back home by bus, I join him.' / 'When I'll have my next holiday, I might go to the seaside.' *(he goes / I'll join, I have)*
- how to complete these sentences? 'If the weather's nice tomorrow, …' 'As soon as I get home today, …' *(students' own answers)*
- the words that mean: 'to have a good knowledge of computers'; 'to have no time left'; 'a free-time activity'? *(computer savvy, I've run out of time, a pastime)*
- the difference between a balanced and a one-sided article? *(A balanced article/essay contains both sides, the pros and the cons, of the argument, but a one-sided article/essay views the topic from only one side.)*
- a phrase you can use for your conclusion in articles? *(the advantages outweigh the disadvantages)*

Progress check

After completing the Summary page questions, encourage students to go back to the Objectives at the beginning of the chapter and assess their learning progress. Students should use the symbols suggested in the Progress check box. This can be followed up in tutorial time with individual students.

Chapter 5 – Worksheet 1
Future clauses

1 If she stays in the sun for too long,	she'll get sunburnt.
2 If it rains,	I'll stay at home.
3 If he asks you,	don't tell him anything.
4 If you touch that broken glass,	you'll cut yourself.
5 Unless you leave the house on time,	you'll miss the train.
6 If he doesn't do his homework,	his teacher will be angry.
7 If you don't eat up,	you can't have any sweets.
8 If we don't take an umbrella,	we might get wet.
9 I won't call him again	if he doesn't answer the phone this time.
10 As soon as I finish my IGCSEs,	I'll take a long holiday.
11 If you eat all that ice-cream,	you'll be sick.
12 If you don't feel well tomorrow,	you should stay at home.
13 If you don't have enough money,	why do you want to buy a new iPad?
14 Until she learns to speak English very well,	she won't be able to study abroad.

Chapter 5 – Worksheet 2
Phrasal verbs with *up* and *out*

run out of something	have no more of something left
bring up somebody	look after somebody and teach them what is right and wrong, when they are little, until they become an adult
grow up	become an adult
go out	leave the house and go to places where you entertain yourself
watch out for something or somebody	be careful
make something up	invent something that is not true or real (e.g. a story)
work something out	think of a solution
give up something	stop doing something for ever
fall out with somebody	have an argument with somebody and stop talking to them
come up with something	think of an idea
look something up	find information

Find somebody who …

1 looks up words in an English dictionary. (how often)
2 has recently fallen out with somebody. (why)
3 grew up in a big city. (where exactly / a good or bad experience)
4 wants to give up something. (what/why)
5 often runs out of time. (when last)

Chapter 6
Art traditions

Reading

Pre-reading activity

Students work in pairs or small groups and discuss the art in each picture, where they think it comes from and whether they like this type of art. Also encourage students to talk about art from their country.

Answers:

1 henna: the Arabic world, India and Pakistan
2 a Mayan artefact: Mexico and Central America
3 an Aboriginal dot painting: Australia
4 a Persian rug: Iran
5 totem poles: North America
6 a fan: Japan

Reading: activity 1

Ask students to scan both texts in 'Surviving art traditions' and find what type of art each text describes and which country/region it originated from.

Answers:

- Text A – *totem poles / along the Pacific coast*
- Text B – *henna / Pakistan, India, Africa and the Middle East*

Vocabulary 1

Exercise 1

Ask students why guessing unknown words from the context is an important skill and what helps them in the text when guessing. If students struggle, ask them to look at the Study tip box in Chapter 2.

Students work in two groups, A and B. Group A tries to guess the words from Text A and group B from Text B. Monitor this stage and check that students have the right ideas.

Then students from group A work with those from group B and exchange ideas.

Exercise 2

Students match the definitions to the correct highlighted word. Check with the class.

Answers:

Text A	Text B
1 tribes	*1 soles*
2 plains	*2 to fade away*
3 to convey	*3 a shrub*
4 decay/rot	*4 to bind to*
5 a hole	*5 to soak*
6 pride	*6 to wilt*
7 to pass down	*7 a stain*
8 to carve	*8 dye*

Reading: activity 2

Students work on their own. Encourage them to highlight the key words in the questions first. Then students read the two texts and answer the questions. They check in pairs before checking with the whole class.

Answers:

A They did not have trees to carve.
B *Any two from:* They take a great deal of work. / They take a great deal of craftsmanship. / They take time to produce.
C singing / dancing to drums
D *Any two from:* the carver's position in his own family / the carver's position in his tribe / pride in his tribe / traditions / tribal life
E They could not afford jewellery.
F heat up to 50 ° C / grows better in dry soil
G It acts as a sunblock / helps to prevent sun's harmful rays from damaging the skin
H flowers and seeds

Reading: activity 3

Draw students' attention to the Study tip box about graphs and charts. Tell them that they will have to extract information from these in exercise 2 of the reading paper. Students work in pairs. They look at the graphs and charts and answer the questions below them. Check the answers with the whole class.

Answers:

Popularity of school subjects among 15 year-olds at the Riverside College

1 2015

2 2013

3 Maths

Free time activities

4 sports

5 computer games

6 girls

Number of people visiting the City Museum

7 December

8 January and February

9 1000

> **Extra idea**
>
> Collect a range of diagrams, including graphs and charts from various sources. Students work with a chart in pairs. They think of a few questions and write them down. They then swap these with the pair next to them and answer the other pair's questions.
>
> **Alternatively:**
>
> Prepare a few questions yourself, one for each graph/chart. Put up the graphs/charts round the room. Each student should have a piece of paper to write their answers on. Read the questions one by one. Students try to locate the information as quickly as possible and write down the answer. At the end students compare their answers in pairs before checking with whole class.
>
> *This activity requires enough physical space in the classroom for students to move around. It is also a good idea to have two sets (or even more depending on the size of the class) of the same graphs/charts so that students don't have to cram round the same graph when looking for the answers.*

Speaking

Speaking: activity 1

Introduce the idea of using certain phrases in English to give yourself a few seconds to think.

Elicit the correct words missing from the four sentences in activity 1. Write the sentences on the board.

Answers:

1 thought

2 see

3 tricky

4 put

Play Track 11 (Transcript 10) and check the answers.

Ask students to look at the Study tip box about sentence stress.

Then play the recording again and ask students if any words are stressed more than others.

Play the recording again; students mark the words that are stressed.

Play the recording one more time, pause after each sentence and practise the sentence stress together.

Answers:

1 I haven't really thought about that.

2 Let me see.

3 Oh, that's a tricky question.

4 How can I put this?

The stressed words in sentences are either the most important words or the words the speaker wants the listener to hear.

Speaking: activity 2

Students work in small groups and discuss the questions. Encourage them to use the phrases from activity 1 during the discussion.

> **Extra idea**
>
> Other ways of practising discussions in class:
>
> - Two students agree to discuss one of the questions. When another student guesses which question is being discussed, they write it on a piece of paper and show it to the pair. If it is the correct topic, the third person joins the discussion and so on.
> - A 'changing circle' discussion. Students start discussing a question in groups. After a minute, ask one student from each group to join another group. The discussion continues with the new member first summarising what the first group agreed on.
> - A 'pyramid' discussion. Students start discussing a question in pairs. They then form a bigger group with another pair and share how they feel about each other's opinions and agree or disagree with the other pair's opinion.

Project

Ask students to think about a painting or a photo that they like or is very special to them. For homework, students prepare a short talk about this picture/photo. Encourage students to bring a copy/printout of it to school, if possible. Students explain why this picture/photo is special, what it shows and how it makes them feel. At the end, other students describe their feelings and reactions to all the pictures.

> **Extra idea**
> Students tell each other about the last time they went to a gallery or museum. For homework, students write a letter to a gallery/museum to request a guided tour for their class outing. Elicit the information needed for such a visit with the whole class.

Language focus

Active or passive?

Analysis

Ask students if they remember what the passive voice is and to give you a few examples. Then ask students to look at the two sentences in bold taken from Text A. Students work in pairs and answer the questions.

Answers:

1 *students' own answer*

2 **Many Native American Indians expressed themselves with their artwork ...** *We only use the main verb which can change according to tense.*

Ropes are used to raise the pole into place. *We use the verb 'to be' and the main verb. The main verb is in the past participle form (used). The verb 'to be' changes according to tense, but the main verb stays the same (i.e. the past participle form).*

3 Sentence A – the active voice; Sentence B – the passive voice.

4 Sentence A.

5 Sentence B.

Ask students to scan read Text A again and find more examples of the passive and active voice. They look at the examples they found in pairs and answer the questions. Discuss answers together.

Answers:

1 The passive voice.

2 The active voice.

3 The passive voice.

4 Examples include newspaper articles, reports, formal letters, etc.

5 The active voice.

Practice

Exercise 1

Do this exercise with the class. Ask students to identify the verb form and the voice.

Answers:

1 He's gone home. *active (Note that the past participle form here is used as part of the present perfect)*

2 This picture was painted a long time ago. *passive (past simple)*

3 I painted my room light green. *active (past simple)*

4 It'll be done as soon as we can. *passive (future)*

5 She was running down the street when she saw him. *active (past continuous) / active (past simple)*

6 I want to be corrected every time I make a mistake. *active (present simple) / passive (infinitive form) / active (present simple)*

7 I corrected all the mistakes in my homework. *active (past simple)*

8 I haven't done the washing up yet. *active (present perfect simple)*

9 It's done very quickly. *passive (present simple)*

10 She's done something silly again. *active (present perfect)*

Note: any perfect continuous form in the active voice (e.g. I've been working on this project for two hours*) can only be changed into the present perfect simple in the passive (e.g.* the project has been worked on for two hours*). There is NO perfect continuous passive form.*

Exercise 2

Ask students to work in pairs and decide whether they need the active or the passive voice. They then complete each gap with the correct form of the verbs.

Answers:

1 was looking / remembered / it was taken (had been taken)

2 was built / was funded

3 was put / worked

4 was painted / thought

5 come
6 is seen
7 is shown
8 try (are trying)
9 be encouraged
10 is going to take off
11 was damaged

Exercise 3

Students work in pairs and scan the first paragraph about henna in Text B. Elicit what form is mostly used and why.

Then ask students to rewrite the paragraph using the passive voice where possible. At the end students display their rewritten paragraphs and compare their answers with others. Choose one answer and discuss it as a class. Encourage peer correction where necessary.

Answers:

It is mostly in the active voice. It tells us what people did with henna. The use of the active voice also makes the paragraph less formal.

Note: Examples of the active voice are underlined. The answers rewritten in the passive voice are in bold.

The art of henna (called 'Mehndi' in Hindi and Urdu) has been practised for over 5000 years in Pakistan, India, Africa and the Middle East. Some documentation has been found relating to this art form that is over 9000 years old. Because henna has natural cooling properties, people of the desert have been using it for centuries **henna has been used by people of the desert for centuries** to cool down their bodies. They make a paste with henna **A paste is made with henna** and soak their palms and the soles of their feet **their palms and the soles of their feet are soaked** in it to get an air-conditioning effect. They feel its cooling sensation **Its cooling sensation is felt** throughout the body for as long as the henna stain remains on their skin. Originally, it was noticed that as the stain faded away, it left patterns on the surface of the skin **patterns were left on the surface of the skin** which led to ideas for making decorative designs. In ancient Egypt, mummies were decorated with henna designs and it is documented that Cleopatra herself used henna as decoration **henna was used by Cleopatra herself as decoration**. Henna was used not only by the rich, but also by the poor, who could not afford jewellery and so used henna **henna was used** to decorate their bodies.

Activate your English

Ask students to think about some traditional art. This could be from the region/country they come from. Set this research for homework. Students write a short paragraph, including the information in the bullet points. Remind them to use the passive voice where possible. As a starting point, discuss some examples of traditional types of art in class and ask students to choose one. (The writing part of this activity could be done for homework).

Students read out their paragraph without naming the type of art. Other students listen and guess what type of art is being presented.

Extra activity

Worksheet 1

The passive and active voice (Information gap / question formation)

Divide the class into two groups, A and B. Each group has the same worksheet. The text is the same for both groups. Each worksheet, however, has different pieces of information missing. Each group has to write down the correct question to obtain this information, using either the active or the passive voice. When each group has finished, check the questions. One student from group A then works with a student from group B, and they take it in turns to ask and answer the questions.

Complete text:

'Photography' is derived from the Greek words 'photos' ('light') and 'graphein' ('to draw'). The word was first used by the scientist Sir John F.W. Herschel in 1839. It is a method of recording images by the action of light on a sensitive material. On a summer day in 1827, Joseph Nicephore Niepce made the first photographic image with a camera obscura. However, Niepce's photograph required eight hours of light exposure to create and after appearing would soon fade away.

Louis Daguerre was also experimenting to find a way to capture an image, but it would take him another dozen years before he was able to reduce exposure time to less than 30 minutes and keep the image from disappearing afterwards. In 1839, after several years of experimentation, Daguerre developed a more convenient and effective method of photography, naming it after himself – 'the daguerreotype'. In 1839, Daguerre and Niepce's son sold the rights for the daguerreotype to the French government and published a booklet describing the process. The daguerreotype gained popularity quickly; by 1850, there were over seventy daguerreotype studios in New York City alone.

Commercial colour films were brought to the market in the early 1940s, with the exception of Kodachrome, which was introduced in 1935.

http://inventors.about.com/od/pstartinventions/a/stilphotography.htm

Answers:

Student A questions:

1 What language is the word 'photography' derived from?
2 How many hours of light exposure did Niepce's photograph require?
3 Who was also experimenting to find a way to capture an image?
4 In 1839, who did Daguerre and Niepce's son sell the rights for the daguerreotype to?
5 In which city were there over 70 daguerreotype studios?

Student B questions:

1 When was the word 'photography' first used?
2 Who made the first photographic image with a camera obscura?
3 When did Daguerre develop a more convenient and effective method of photography?
4 What did Daguerre and Niepce's son publish in 1839?
5 What type of films was brought to the market in the early 1940s?

Listening 1

Pre-listening activity

Introduce the topic of face painting. For students who are unfamiliar with face painting, draw their attention to the picture in the Coursebook. Ask students to work in small groups and think of as many different uses of face painting as possible. Give students a time limit to do this activity. Elicit one or two examples from the class (e.g. Native Americans, make-up, etc.).

Listening: activity 1

Ask students to listen to the recording and write down the uses of face painting introduced in the recording. Students compare their lists in pairs before checking with the whole class.

Answers:

From: drawing on a child's face / a way of camouflaging for hunting or fighting purposes / in religious ceremonies / part of entertainment (e.g. the opera) / in sports (e.g. American football, wrestling)

Vocabulary 2

Before doing the exam-type listening exercise in activity 2, students look up the words in an English dictionary.

Listening: activity 2

Introduce the exam-type listening exercise. Remind students of the best way to tackle this question. This includes looking through the notes with the gaps and trying to predict the type of answers needed. Play the recording (Transcript 11), students listen and fill in the gaps in the notes. Students should not use more than two words per gap. Play the recording twice as in the exam.

Answers:

a fun
b natural environment
c symbols
d special powers
e costumes
f Wrestling
g fans
h 1980

Vocabulary 3

Exercise 1

Help students to remember what a collocation and a fixed phrase is by asking them to look back at the Key term box in Chapter 2. Students look through Transcript 11 and complete the missing word in each collocation / fixed phrase. This could be done as a competition in class or as homework.

Exercise 2

When checking the answers to Exercise 1, encourage students to identify the words used in each collocation (e.g. verb and noun, adjective and noun, etc.)

Answers to Exercises 1 and 2:

1 to think <u>about</u> *(verb and preposition)*
2 to date <u>back</u> *(verb and preposition)*
3 a <u>wide</u> variety of *(fixed phrase, adjective and noun)*
4 to be aware <u>of</u> *(adjective and preposition)*
5 good <u>for</u> *(adjective and preposition)*
6 would be <u>less</u> likely to do something *(fixed phrase, adverb and adverb)*
7 in the <u>natural</u> environment *(adjective and noun)*
8 to <u>become</u> common *(verb and adjective)*

9 to be associated with something *(verb and preposition)*

10 to participate in *(verb and preposition)*

11 it wasn't until about the 1980s *(fixed phrase)*

12 as a way for somebody to enjoy themselves *(fixed expression)*

Exercise 3

Students work in pairs and rewrite the sentences using the most suitable phrase from Exercise 1.

Encourage peer correction where necessary. When all questions are correct, students choose three to ask other students.

Answers:

A What are you less likely to do this weekend?

B What became common in your life after you joined this school?

C What do you think about modern art?

D What do you need to be aware of when living in a big city?

E What is art good for?

F Do you participate in creative projects? Give examples.

Writing

Pre-writing activity

Students work in small groups and talk about the four photographs.

Writing: activity 1

First students read the exam-type question and underline key words. Remind students of the need to stay within the word limit.

Students then read a sample answer and say if Arturo chose one of the four photographs given or a different one. Students read the sample answer again and underline Arturo's answers to the exam question.

Note that there are some intentional errors that are dealt with in activity 3.

- Say where it was taken: *It was taken outside Takeshi's grandmother's house.*
- Say when it was taken: *It was taken last month / when visiting Takeshi / one afternoon.*
- Describe the photograph: *There's Takeshi's grandmother with her cat. Each of the cat's eyes had a different colour.*
- Say why you chose it for the competition: *It showed the difference in mood between the grandmother and the cat quite well.*

Writing: activity 2

This activity raises students' awareness of the assessment criteria for any writing exercises that are in their exam. Explain to students that they are assessed on content and language. Draw students' attention to the Key term box explaining what content is. Explain that both content and language are equally important to get good marks.

Ask students to look at the list of the assessment areas. Explain the terms carefully to make sure students understand the meanings of these words. Students then work in pairs and put the terms under the correct heading for content or language. Do the first two together as an example.

Answers:

- **Content:** *answering the question fully, developing ideas, appropriate register, appropriate length*
- **Language:** *grammar, punctuation, tenses, range of vocabulary, spelling, well-organised paragraphs, linkers*

Writing: activity 3

Students scan Arturo's letter and underline all the mistakes they can find. Elicit from the class which areas Arturo needs to improve, i.e. *tenses (grammar) and spelling.*

Students then work in pairs and look at the mistakes they underlined and correct them.

Answers:

Hi Simon,

Hope everything is good your end. Sorry I haven't been in touch for so long, but I've been really busy with my photography *obsession* and with the school photography competition.

You'll never believe this, but I won the competition. One of my photos won the first prize. I was really *thrilled* because I didn't expect that at all, to tell you the truth.

Anyway, let me tell you about the photo. I took it last month when I was visiting my friend Takeshi. I'm sure I told you about him. We *studied* English together in Malta and then stayed in touch. He invited me to stay with him and his grandmother. She's in the picture, actually. I took it one afternoon outside their house. She had this crazy cat which kept jumping on people's *shoulders*. Plus, each of the cat's eyes had a *different* colour. I've never seen anything like it. They made a funny *pair*. The grandma looks happy in this photo and the cat looks really grumpy. I *thought* the photo showed the mood of the two quite well and that's why I felt it would stand out in the competition. What do you *reckon*?

Apart from that, nothing much has happened. What about you? Any news?

Take care and drop me a line when you can.

Arturo

Vocabulary 4

After the sample answer has been corrected, ask students to scan the letter and find synonymous words/phrases to those in this exercise. This exercise could also be done for homework.

Answers:

1 an obsession
2 You'll never believe this, but …
3 thrilled
4 to tell you the truth
5 Anyway,
6 to stay in touch
7 Plus,
8 I've never seen anything like it
9 grumpy
10 What do you reckon?
11 drop me a line

Writing: activity 4

Ask students to write their own letter in response to the same task as in activity 1. They can choose one of the four photos or a photo they took themselves. This activity could be done for homework. Encourage students to use some of the new vocabulary and to proofread their work after they have finished.

Writing: activity 5

Ask students to swap their answers and discuss together which parts of the letter are well written and identify some areas for improvement.

Extra activity

Worksheet 2

Error correction

Students work in small groups and correct the mistakes. Encourage student–student interaction when discussing the mistakes. Each group is given ten points to start with. When checking answers, students are given a point for correct answers, but lose a point if the correction is wrong.

Answers:

1 I have never liked rainy weather. (*wrong order*)
2 Can you tell me what the time is? (*indirect question*)
3 I've been working on this project for the past two days and I still haven't finished. (*tense – grammar*)
4 When I go swimming, I always take my cousin with me. (*spelling*)
5 He's such a grumpy person. I don't like talking to/with him. (*wrong words*)
6 I've been thinking of going for a holiday in India. (*a missing article and a wrong article*)
7 I can't see you tomorrow. I'm busy with my homework. *(wrong word (preposition) / grammar – countable/ uncountable nouns)*
8 If he helps me, I can finish early and go home. *(grammar – subject/verb agreement / punctuation)*
9 How long have you known your best friend? *(tense – grammar)*
10 I went to Peru last year. We planned the journey very carefully. *(tense – grammar / spelling)*

Listening 2

Listening: activity 1

Students look at the questions. Ask them to circle or underline the key words. Remind them that they need to write up to three words for each answer. Also, remind them that some answers require two details or two examples. Play each recording twice.

Students check answers in pairs before checking with the whole class.

Answers:

1 **a** next week
b Monday(s)
2 **a** (his) neighbour
b chocolate cake

3 **a** National Geographic
b $/5.50

4 **a** 6.30 OR half past six OR 6.30p.m. OR 18.30
b French posters

Listening: activity 2

Explain to students that there is some distracting information in the recording and why this is included. (Students are expected to be able to discriminate between relevant and irrelevant details.)

Students look at the words which are the distractors taken from each recording (e.g. days /times, etc.). Then they listen again to each recording and discuss why the information is wrong.

This exercise could also be used as a reading activity with Transcript 12.

See Transcript 12 for answers.

Summary page

Students work in pairs and answer the questions.

Alternatively:

Students work in small groups without looking at the Summary page. Read out the questions one at a time. For each question students agree on the right answer. They either answer from memory, or look up the answer in the chapter. The whole group has to agree on the correct answer. Each group nominates one student to write their answers on the board. Award a point for each correct answer.

Go through all the answers with the whole class at the end of the competition so that all students have the correct answers.

Can you remember …

Answers:

- **three** types of traditional art from around the world? *(See answers for pre-reading activity in Teacher's Book.)*
- which words, from the following selection, go with 'totem poles' and which ones with 'henna'? The words are: 'a hole', 'soles', 'shrub', 'plains', 'decay', 'to wilt' and 'to fade away'. *('Totem poles': a hole, plains, decay. 'Henna': soles, shrub, to wilt, to fade away)*
- **two** phrases you can use to give yourself more time to think when you are discussing something? *(any two from: I haven't really thought about that; Let me see …; Oh, that's a tricky question; How can I put this?)*
- why we use the passive voice in some situations rather than the active voice? Give **two** reasons. *(We are more interested in the activity that takes place [e.g. when describing processes] rather than the person who carries out the activity [e.g. when narrating a story]. We also use it to make the sentence more formal and impersonal [e.g. formal letters, essays, reports, etc.].)*
- how to change sentences in the active voice into the passive voice? Can you rewrite the following sentences in the passive voice? 'I'm going to clean my room tomorrow.' 'I took this photo last month.' *(My room is going to be cleaned tomorrow. This photo was taken last month.)*
- **three** examples of situations when people paint, or painted, their faces? *(for example: Native Americans, for performances [theatre, circus], for camouflage, in sport [wrestling, football fans], etc.)*
- what prepositions you need in the following collocations: 'to think … '; to date … '; 'to be aware … something'? *(to think about, to date back, to be aware of something)*
- what you are assessed on in the written exercises in the exam? What are the two categories? *(content and language)*
- at least one example for each category in the previous question? *(**Content:** answering the question fully, developing ideas, appropriate register, appropriate length. **Language:** grammar, punctuation, tenses, range of vocabulary, spelling, well-organised paragraphs, idioms, linkers.)*
- what you should do when you have finished your writing? *(read it again, i.e. proofread it)*
- the words that mean: 'in a bad mood'; 'a strong interest in something'? *(grumpy; an obsession)*

Progress check

After completing the Summary page questions, encourage students to go back to the Objectives at the beginning of the chapter and assess their learning progress. Students should use the symbols suggested in the Progress check box. This can be followed up in tutorial time with individual students.

Chapter 6 – Worksheet 1

The passive and active voice (information gap / question formation)

Student A

A brief history of photography

'Photography' is derived from the (1) .... words 'photos' (light) and 'graphein' (to draw). The word was first used by the scientist Sir John F.W. Herschel in 1839. It is a method of recording images by the action of light on a sensitive material. On a summer day in 1827, Joseph Nicephore Niepce made the first photographic image with a camera obscura. However, Niepce's photograph required (2)......................... hours of light exposure to create and after appearing would soon fade away.

(3)................................ was also experimenting to find a way to capture an image, but it would take him another dozen years before he was able to reduce exposure time to less than 30 minutes and keep the image from disappearing afterwards. In 1839, after several years of experimentation, Daguerre developed a more convenient and effective method of photography, naming it after himself – 'the daguerreotype'. In 1839, Daguerre and Niepce's son sold the rights for the daguerreotype to the (4)......................... .... and published a booklet describing the process. The daguerreotype gained popularity quickly; by 1850, there were over seventy daguerreotype studios in (5).................................... alone.

Commercial colour films were brought to the market in the early 1940s, with the exception of Kodachrome, which was introduced in 1935.

http://inventors.about.com/od/pstartinventions/a/stilphotography.htm

Student B

A brief history of photography

'Photography' is derived from the Greek words 'photos' (light) and 'graphein' ('to draw'). The word was first used by the scientist Sir John F.W. Herschel in (1) .... It is a method of recording images by the action of light on a sensitive material. On a summer day in 1827, (2).................. made the first photographic image with a camera obscura. However, Niepce's photograph required eight hours of light exposure to create and after appearing would soon fade away.

Louis Daguerre was also experimenting to find a way to capture an image, but it would take him another dozen years before he was able to reduce exposure time to less than 30 minutes and keep the image from disappearing afterwards. In (3)......................, after several years of experimentation, Daguerre developed a more convenient and effective method of photography, naming it after himself – 'the daguerreotype'. In 1839, Daguerre and Niepce's son sold the rights for the daguerreotype to the French government and published a (4)...................... describing the process. The daguerreotype gained popularity quickly; by 1850, there were over seventy daguerreotype studios in New York City alone.

(5).. films were brought to the market in the early 1940s, with the exception of Kodachrome, which was introduced in 1935.

http://inventors.about.com/od/pstartinventions/a/stilphotography.htm

Chapter 6 – Worksheet 2
Error correction

Can you spot the mistake in each sentence? Sometimes there is more than one mistake. Write the corrected sentences.

1 I never have liked rainy weather.

....

2 Can you tell me what's the time?

....

3 I was working on this project for the past two days and I still haven't finished.

....

4 When I go swiming, I always take my cosin with me.

....

5 He's so a grumpy person. I don't like talking at him.

....

6 I've been thinking of going for holiday in the India.

....

7 I can't see you tomorrow. I'm busy for my homeworks.

....

8 If he help me I can finish early and go home.

....

9 How long have you been knowing your best friend?

....

10 I've been to Peru last year. We planned the journey very carefully.

....

Chapter 7
Sports and games

Reading

Pre-reading activity

In small groups students try to name the sports in the pictures. Elicit the names (the answers are the subheadings in the reading text), but don't let them look at the text at this point. Put the names of the sports on the board. Ask students to discuss the questions in this activity in groups. Elicit a few answers from each group.

Reading: activity 1

Ask students what they think the sports have in common. Don't give them the correct answer. Elicit a few different opinions.

Ask students to read the opening paragraph and check answers with the whole class. Ask students what 'bidding for a place' in the title means.

Vocabulary 1

Students work in pairs and try to guess the meaning of the words from the context. Don't allow the use of dictionaries at this point. Ask students to look at the highlighted words in the text and read the sentence before and after the highlighted words. Students should look for clues in the text that will help them to guess the meaning of these words. Guiding questions are added to help students to look at the right clues.

Do one word as an example with the class. Then each pair does all words and answers the guiding questions in this exercise. Check answers with the class. If students guess the words correctly, there is no need to use the dictionary. If students fail to guess the correct meaning, ask them to look the word up in an English dictionary to check the correct meaning.

Extra idea

- If resources allow, it is a good idea to have an online dictionary available for the whole class to see the correct definitions if necessary.
- 'Dictionary duty': at the start of each lesson, nominate one or two students who will look up words in the online dictionary for others to see when necessary. If an online dictionary is not available, a printed one could be used instead.

Answers:

Introductory paragraph

re- means again, or repeated

Inline speed skating

- It is followed by a place (Northern Europe). A 'root' means the beginning of something, where it originates from.
- 'Include' means the opposite of exclude. Exclude has a negative meaning – not to be included.

Softball and baseball

- 'Joint' refers to two sports, softball and baseball. The sentence says: 'the bid is for both sports'.
- 'Tackle one obstacle' – an 'obstacle' is something difficult, a problem (here it is the absence of professional players); we want to change it because having professional players is very important to success in the Olympic bid.

Sport climbing

They are attached to the climbing wall and climbers hold on to them, or stand on them while climbing.

Squash

The verb is to 'include'. They are trying to make sure that squash is part of the Olympic Games.

Wakeboarding

The board / the participants are moved across water. A boat / cable system / trucks are used. The synonym is 'be pulled by'.

Wushu

- Two categories are mentioned. 'The former' refers to the first mentioned category.
- Lose points; it says '... for any mistakes that appear ...'. Participants wouldn't gain points for making mistakes, quite the opposite.

Reading: activity 2

Ask students to look at the questions first and identify the key words. Then students read the text and answer the questions. To help students prepare for an exam, it is useful to give a time limit to complete the question.

> **TEACHING TIP**
> - When doing exam practice or exam past papers, encourage students to keep a record of the time it takes them to complete each exam exercise (reading or writing). Review this periodically in tutorials. Suggest ways of improving students' reading/writing speed.
> - Encourage students to use text with headings to their advantage to locate information more quickly. Also, answers should be brief and concise.

Answers:

1 burn as many calories as with running / gentler on your joints
2 the throat
3 bigger ball / shorter bat / smaller pitch *(any **two** for a mark)*
4 the absence of professional players
5 permanently fixed anchors
6 cables (attached to machines)
7 the moves / 'taolu'

> **Extra idea**
> To practise scanning a text, choose any text of your choice and prepare a few questions. Read out the questions to the students. Students work in teams and try to locate the information faster than the other team. When students locate the answer, they write it on the board. If the answer is correct, that team scores a point. If not, other teams continue looking for the correct answer until one of them finds it.

Speaking

Speaking: activity 1

In small groups, students decide which three sports from the pictures in the pre-reading activity they want to include in the 2020 Olympic Games. Encourage them to give reasons for their opinions. Then all groups compare their answers together and explain their choices.

Note that in September 2013, it was decided not to include any of these sports at the Tokyo Olympics in 2020. Instead, wrestling was included in the Olympics. It was brought back in response to strong opposition in many countries against an earlier decision not to include it in the Olympic bid.

Speaking: activity 2

Students work in small groups and discuss the questions. Elicit a few answers and encourage a whole class discussion.

Select a few questions which could be used as an exam-type writing question and ask students to write an article for homework. The ideas should come from their discussion with other students.

> **Extra idea**
> **Carousel**
> Copy the questions and cut them up into three sets. Put one set of questions on each table. Students move round in groups. Set a time limit of a few minutes for each set of questions.
>
> **Alternatively:** If this set-up is not possible, give each group a set of questions to start with. After the time is up, ask each group to pass on their sets clockwise. Students carry on in this manner until they have discussed all the sets.

Vocabulary 2

Ask students if they can remember what 'vocabulary sets' are and why they are important. Draw students' attention to Chapter 3.

Exercise 1

Tell students they are going to focus on vocabulary sets based round different sports. Divide the class into three groups. Each group looks at one sport (i.e. karate, squash, softball) and completes the diagram. Ask them to check the meaning of any unknown words.

Give students a large sheet of paper and ask them to make a wall poster of the diagram with their answers. Monitor to check that answers are correct. Students then share their words with the whole class. Encourage other students to ask their peers for clarification of the meaning of the words.

Note that the number of lines in each diagram doesn't indicate the number of correct answers. There are more answers than there are lines.

Suggested answers:

- **Softball:** *a bat, a ball, a game, a pitch*
- **Karate:** *martial art, punches, kicks, sweeps, fight, a mat, target the opponent, hit above the belt*
- **Squash:** *players, hit a ball, a racket, hit the front wall, miss the ball*

Note that alternatives are possible.

Exercise 2

Students work in groups of three. Each student talks about the sport they chose for exercise 1. For example: Student A – karate, etc. Each student has to talk for one minute (or longer). Give students 2–3 minutes to prepare what they want to say, but don't let them write anything down (as in the speaking exam). Encourage them to use as many words from the diagram as they can. Then each student talks for one minute. When the time is up, the other two students should ask questions about what has been said and develop a group discussion. Allow a few minutes for this.

Listening 1

Listening: activity 1

Ask students why they think 'vocabulary sets' are important for their listening skills. Elicit a few ideas. Then ask them to read the Study tip box to compare their answers.

Students look at the list of sports before they listen and tell each other what they know about each one. Explain any unfamiliar sports from the list, but don't give away too much related vocabulary from the listening exercise. Students listen and match the correct sport to each speaker. Play twice if necessary. Students compare their answers before checking with the whole class.

Answers:

- Speaker 1: *volleyball*
- Speaker 2: *badminton*
- Speaker 3: *ice hockey*

Listening: activity 2

Students listen again and write down as many related words for each sport as they can. Ask three students to write their selection on the board. Then play the recording again and stop each time a related word comes up. Check with the whole class that it is on the list on the board.

If students struggle to identify the words in the audio recording, ask them to read Transcript 13.

Answers:

- Volleyball: *team sport, hitting the ball, net, keep the ball off the ground, the court*
- Badminton: *doubles game, hit the shuttlecock, umpire*
- Ice hockey: *dangerous sport, fall, harder landing, the puck, a helmet, the goalkeeper, protective shield, stick*

Extra activity

Worksheet 1

Guessing game

Part 1:
Cut up the top half of the worksheet with names of sports. Students work in groups. Each student picks the top card and describes/explains the sport on the card using related vocabulary, but not mentioning the name of the sport. Other students try to guess the sport. If the student is not familiar with the sport, they can pick another card. Set a time limit of ten minutes. At the end, the team with most correct answers wins.

For homework, students can look up related vocabulary for the sports they were unfamiliar with.

Part 2:
Students look at the second half of the worksheet and categorise the words/phrases. You will need one set of cards for each pair/group and also the worksheet as a whole for each student to write the answers in after they have been checked with the whole class.

This vocabulary worksheet could also be done for homework and done as a guessing game in the following lesson to check if students can remember the meaning of the words/phrases.

Answers:

- Phrasal verbs: *turn up, fall out with, make up with, get over*
- Injuries: *a bruise, a bump on the head, a sprained ankle, a broken wrist*
- Problems in the house: *a burst pipe, a power cut, I got locked out, a stain on the carpet*
- Ways of walking: *wander, plod, limp, rush*
- Synonyms for 'happy': *excited, over the moon, thrilled, pleased*
- Synonyms for 'unhappy': *grumpy, sulky, in a bad mood, irritable*

Follow-on activity:
Students write up a narrative using as many of the words and phrases as they can. This could be done as an exam-type writing task.

A letter to a friend:

- What happened to you.
- Where and when.
- How you felt at the start.
- How you felt at the end.

Project

Students should work in six groups or pairs. Each group is given one unusual sport from the selection in their books. For homework they should research the sport (e.g. how it's played, who plays it, how many players, where, equipment needed, etc.) and write a short summary. Draw students' attention to the useful phrases section.

It is a good idea to think of the main points to focus on in class time. If Internet access is available to students, the research could be done in class time. Ask students to bring in a picture of the sport, if possible.

In the following lesson, put the names of the sports on the board with a picture. Students give presentations about their sport to other students, who have to guess which sport is being described. Encourage students to ask questions at the end of each presentation.

Students work in groups and have a discussion at the end.

Ask students to write a letter to a local gym enquiring about joining. Before students attempt their answers, elicit the audience, style and register. Students discuss in pairs how they would organise their ideas. Students write their letter in class, or for homework. Alternatively, students can do a role-play on the phone – enquiring about joining a gym.

Features of the letter:

- audience – a gym manager / a gym receptionist
- style – an enquiry letter
- register – semi-formal to formal (the letter is intended for somebody in charge of the gym, somebody we don't know)
- organisation – suggest three paragraphs (paragraph 1 – introduction, reason for writing; paragraph 2 – asking questions; paragraph 3 – thanking for replying)

Listening 2

Pre-listening activity 1

Students work in groups and do the quiz about the Olympic Games. Award one point for each correct answer.

Quiz answers:

A *Pierre de Coubertin*

B *France*

C *1896 (Summer)/1924 (Winter)*

D *Athens (Summer) / Chamonix, France (Winter)*

E *No*

F *Every 4 years*

G *8 cities:*

Summer: Athens, Paris, Los Angeles, London (3x), Stockholm

Winter: Lake Placid (USA), St. Moritz (Switzerland), Innsbruck (Austria)

H *Athens (2004), Beijing (2008), London (2012), Rio de Janeiro (2016)*

I *Lausanne, Switzerland*

J *Olympia, Greece*

Pre-listening activity 2

Introduce the topic of 'Paralympics'. Ask students if they are familiar with the term and if they know any Paralympians.

Vocabulary 3

Before students listen to the recording, check that they understand the words.

Listening: activity 1

Ask students to look at the questions and identify the key words. Students listen and circle the correct answer. Play the recording twice. Ask students to read the transcript for homework to identify the correct answers.

> **TEACHING TIP**
> When practising this type of listening exercise, ask students to look at the questions only while they are listening. They should identify the answer and write it down in their own words. If they identify the correct answer, they should be able to match this with one of the options very easily. This will enable students to focus more on the audio text without having to read all the options whilst listening.

Answers:

1 C

2 C

3 B

4 A

5 C

6 C

7 A

8 A

Language focus

Verb forms

Analysis

Ask students to look at the three sentences and underline the verbs. Go through the categories, make sure students understand what they mean (see the Key term box) and ask them to put the first verbs in the correct category.

Answers:

A He enjoyed watching them getting involved. *('enjoy' is followed by the '-ing' form)*

B … these didn't seem to have the same impact. *('seem' is followed by the infinitive form)*

C He believed that sport could make his patients' lives much better. *('could' [as with most modal verbs] is followed by the bare infinitive)*

Students work in pairs and categorise all the verbs in the box.

Alternatively:

Write the verbs onto cards. Spread the cards over the floor. Students work in three groups. Each group focuses on one verb form group and selects the verbs that belong in their category. Students stick the verbs on the wall for others to see. Check with the whole class to see if they agree with the final selections.

Answers:

- **Infinitive with 'to':** want, decide, offer, hope, ask (somebody), deserve, would prefer, intend, promise
- **Bare infinitive:** should, make (somebody), can, must, let (somebody)
- ***-ing* form:** admit, deny, finish, enjoy, suggest, dislike, practise, keep

Practice

Exercise 1

Students work in pairs and correct the mistakes.

Answers:

1. Suki enjoys to go to the gym a lot. *(going)*
2. Kelly let me to eat her sandwich. *(eat)*
3. Ivan has offered give his best friend all his DVDs. *(to give)*
4. Mohsin promised doing his English homework at the weekend. *(to do)*
5. Faran can running faster than any of his friends. *(run)*
6. Tim asked me phone him tonight. *(to phone)*
7. Ivan admitted to be often late for his swimming lessons. *(being)*
8. I'd prefer going to the seaside this summer. *(to go)*
9. My brother suggested to go to the cinema tonight. What do you think? *(going)*
10. Why don't you ask somebody help you with the project? *(to help)*

Exercise 2

Swap students round so that they work with a different partner and ask them to complete the sentences, orally, with their ideas.

Students write sentences in full for homework.

Alternatively:

Copy the sentence beginnings and cut them up into strips. Students work in groups. Each group selects somebody to get one card at a time from you. Then they take it to the team and complete the sentence in writing. They have to show you their sentence. If there are no mistakes, they can get the next sentence. If the sentence has a mistake in it, they have to take it back to the team and correct it. To ensure that students' sentences are not too short, set a target of five words or more.

The groups continue in this manner until they have completed all the sentences. The first group to finish wins.

Activate your English

Students work in pairs and prepare a questionnaire with five questions. Encourage the use of the verbs practised in the Language section. If time is limited, set the questions for homework. Then they mingle and ask other students their questions. Elicit a few answers at the end.

Extra idea

To practise verb forms and questions/answers, type up the verbs from this section and cut the cards up. Make one set for each group. You will also need a dice for each group. Even numbers mean 'ask a question', odd numbers mean 'make a sentence'. Students take it in turns to throw the dice and to pick a verb. They either have to say a sentence using the verb, or ask somebody a question using the verb.

Reading and writing

Pre-reading activity

First, make sure students understand the meaning of the four words. Also, highlight that 'equipment' is uncountable. Therefore, it doesn't have a plural form and also doesn't take 'an' in the singular form.

Students work in pairs and ask each other questions using the four words. Then they answer each other's questions.

Reading and writing: activity 1

First, elicit the rules when doing this type of exam exercise. If students struggle to come up with the rules, ask them to look back at Chapter 4.

Students look at the form, read the text, find the relevant information and fill in the form. Encourage students to underline the answers.

Reading and writing: activity 2

Students swap their answers in pairs and check. Encourage students to give each other feedback before checking the answers with the whole class. Project the text onto the board, if possible. Ask students to underline the answers in the text on the board.

Answers:

The Tree of Life Gym

Application and Booking Form

Section A: Personal details

Full name: *Christina Aranda*

Address: *14 El Prado Square, Santa Marta, Venezuela*

Age: 16–18 (19–25) 26–35 36–45 over 45 (please circle)

Gender: ~~Male~~/Female (please delete)

Phone number (daytime): *076 77749399*

Emergency contact name and number: *079 33391012 – Irene Aranda*

Section B: Requirements

Will you require a personal trainer? ☑ Yes ☐ No (please tick)

For how many sessions would you like to book your personal trainer? *3 sessions*

Would you like to hire any of the gym exercise equipment? ☑ Yes ☐ No (please tick)

What equipment will you require and for how long? Give details. *treadmill and cross trainer for three months*

Section C

In the space below write **one sentence** stating why you would like to have a personal trainer or not, and **one sentence** giving details of any previous physical injuries we should know about.

Idea one: want to use new exercise machines so need to know how to use them OR need not to overdo the exercise because of previous injuries

Idea two: broken leg, 2 cracked ribs, twisted wrist

(Remind students of the need for full sentences and complete accuracy in grammar and punctuation. For example:

I need a personal trainer to show me how to use the exercise machines. I have broken my leg once.)

Speaking and writing

Speaking and writing activity

Student A fills in the same form, but this time invents their own answers. Student B thinks of questions they will ask as the receptionist. Then they work in pairs and do the role-play – asking questions and providing answers. The receptionist should fill in the form with the answers given. The receptionist should copy the answers, but only listen to get the information required (do not permit students to show the form to their partner). Encourage students to ask each other for clarification when necessary.

It is a good idea to photocopy a blank form for each student from the Coursebook for this activity.

Speaking activity

Students work in groups and discuss the questions. At the end, encourage each group to write a short paragraph about the outcomes of the discussion. Encourage the use of the Useful language 1. Students then read out their paragraphs and discuss the outcomes together with the other groups. This time encourage the use of Useful language 2.

Extra activity

Worksheet 2

Spelling bees

Remind students of the importance of correct spelling when they write. Students work in pairs and test each other's spelling. They take it in turns, pick a card and ask their partner to spell the word. If they spell the word correctly, they get to keep the card. At the end, the student with more cards wins.

Extra idea
Encourage students to keep their own spelling lists of words they often misspell or find difficult to spell.

Summary page

Can you remember …

Students work in small groups and answer the questions. Check with the whole class.

- at least **three** sports that are bidding for a place at the Olympic Summer Games in 2020? *(See the Reading section for answers.)*
- what the noun is from 'to include'? *(inclusion)*
- the words that mean: 'to be pulled by'; 'to originate / to come from'; 'to deal with a problem'? *(to be towed by; to have (its) roots in; to tackle an obstacle)*
- at least **three** words connected with badminton and ice hockey? *(For answers see Transcript 13, speakers 2 and 3.)*
- at least **three** interesting facts about the Olympic Games? *(See the answers for the 'Olympic Games quiz' in the teacher's notes, Listening 2.)*
- at least **four** interesting facts about the Paralympic Games? *(For answers see Transcript 14.)*
- the **three** verb forms you learnt about in this chapter? *(infinitive with 'to', bare infinitive, -ing form)*
- at least **two** examples for each verb form? *(For answers, see Language focus, Analysis section.)*
- what is wrong with the two following sentences? 'My dad never lets stay out late.' 'Our teacher suggested to have a celebration at the end of the term.' *(lets me stay; suggested having)*
- **two** examples of exercise equipment? *(a treadmill, a cross trainer)*
- what a personal trainer is? Write down **two** advantages of having a personal trainer. *(Somebody who advises you and helps you to exercise effectively. Advantages: helps you to put together a personal exercise routine, explains how to use exercising equipment, etc.)*

Progress check

After completing the Summary page questions, encourage students to go back to the Objectives at the beginning of the chapter and assess their learning progress. Students should use the symbols suggested in the Progress check box. This can be followed up in tutorial time with individual students.

Chapter 7 – Worksheet 1

Guessing game – Activity 1:

football	golf	cricket	baseball
basketball	squash	tennis	table tennis
rugby	water polo	boxing	bowling
ski slalom	archery	car racing	snooker
windsurfing	scuba diving	fencing	triathlon

Activity 2:

What are the categories?

Can you put the words into categories and decide what the best name for each category is?

excited	a burst pipe	a broken wrist	in a bad mood
fall out with	grumpy	wander	make up with
I got locked out	a bruise	over the moon	a bump on the head
a sprained ankle	limp	sulky	a power cut
thrilled	turn up	a stain on the carpet	rush
plod	get over	pleased	irritable

Chapter 7 – Worksheet 2
Spelling bees

application	unnecessary	suggest	because	exciting
accident	written	weather	successful	experience
which	further	apply	environment	previous
recommend	beautiful	equipment	familiar	birthday
straight	enough	require	injuries	writing

Chapter 8
Inventions

Reading and writing

Pre-reading activity

In small groups, students discuss important inventions. Each group then decides together on its top five inventions and shares their list with the class. Encourage the students to explain their selections.

In the same groups, students look at the inventions in the photos, answer the questions and express their opinions. Encourage a short discussion.

Vocabulary 1

Students work in two groups. Each group looks up the meaning of the words on their list in an English dictionary. Monitor and help where necessary. Students then explain the meaning of these words to the other group. Check the answers with the class before continuing.

Reading: activity 1

Students scan the text and find the numbers and names. Encourage students to underline the name or number once they have found it. They then read the specific part of the text to find out what the information refers to. Check answers with the class. Encourage paraphrasing.

Possible answers:

1. Spencer Silver – the inventor of the adhesive that was later used on sticky notes, an employee of the 3M company.
2. 100 – the approximate number of countries where sticky notes are sold.
3. 1.8 billion – how many telephone devices were sold in 2013.
4. 2014 – the year it was estimated that the online shopping industry was going to grow to $1.5 trillion globally.
5. 1876 – the year the telephone was invented.
6. Michael Aldrich – the person who is considered to be the inventor of online shopping.
7. 90 per cent – the percentage of companies that decided to purchase more sticky notes from 3M after 3M had handed out free samples for businesses to try out.
8. 1960s – the decade when people didn't believe remote shopping was going to work.
9. William Preece – the leading engineer for the British Post Office who found telephones unnecessary because messenger boys did the same job delivering messages. He thought the telephone was just a novelty that would pass.

Reading: activity 2

Students look at the headings in the exercise and read the text. They decide which information goes under each heading and make notes in the spaces provided.

Answers:

Allow reasonable paraphrasing.

Reasons why some people thought these inventions wouldn't work:

(Any three answers from the following)

- didn't believe in innovations
- they found them strange, unnecessary and impractical
- messenger boys did a good job delivering messages (so why have a telephone?)
- the telephone was a novelty
- nobody could see any practical use for (the adhesive)
- still believed that this invention wasn't going to be commercially successful and people would continue to use scrap paper for their notes rather than sticky notes
- people preferred to see the products they were buying and to handle them in person before they decided to make a purchase (online shopping)
- better telecommunication links to people's homes were needed

Practical difficulties with some of the inventions:

(Any two answers from the following)

- how to make the glue stay on the sticky note itself, rather than peeling off and staying on the surface it was attached to
- length of time it would take to deliver products to the customer, as the shipping speed was very slow
- *inadequate telecommunication*

Examples to show evidence that the inventions are now successful

(Any two answers from the following)

- ... we all have at least one telephone at home and mobile phones have become such a vital part of our lives that we can't imagine going even one day without them.
- Telephones have now developed into mobile, smart and portable devices whose sales reached 1.8 billion units in 2013.
- Sticky notes are commonly used in offices and households throughout the world.
- Sticky notes are sold in more than 100 countries.
- We now buy almost everything online.
- ... estimated that the online shopping industry would grow to $1.5 trillion globally.

TEACHING TIP

When writing notes, it is important to write the answers under the correct heading.

Reading and writing: activity 1

In pairs, students write a summary. A reminder of the rules can be found in the Study tip box in Chapter 5. Explain that some parts of the summary have already been written. Students should use some of the ideas from Reading activity 2 and fit them in the summary template. Ask one pair to do the answer on the board. When checking answers with the whole class, encourage peer correction. This can be done individually or as a pair-work exercise.

TEACHING TIP

Both accuracy of language and relevant content are important. Students need to use their own words as much as possible, with the use of linkers to group ideas in a logical sequence. Answers should be clear, accurate and precise.

Pre-reading activity

Students work in two groups. One group discusses the advantages and the other group discusses the disadvantages of the Internet. Each group should make notes. Check answers with the whole class and encourage a short discussion between the two groups.

Reading and writing: activity 2

Students read the text and complete the notes. Set a time limit for this exam-type activity. Then check answers together.

Alternatively: This exercise can be set for homework.

Answers:

Advantages: getting hold of information quickly; research easier from the comfort of your own home; has brought the world closer together; keeping in touch easier; record anything, anywhere, and at any time and videos instantly posted on YouTube; spared us trouble of going to the bank, supermarkets, shops or colleges; hassle-free shopping online.

Disadvantages: whether information is accurate or reliable; lose privacy; job applicants being rejected because of inappropriate pictures, etc. being made public; shops closing down; identity theft; viruses.

Vocabulary 2

Exercise 1

Students guess the meaning of the highlighted words and word or phrases. Encourage them to read around each phrase and look for clues to help with understanding.

Exercise 2

Students match the definitions to the correct highlighted word or phrase in the text. Students check answers in pairs before checking with the whole class.

Answers:

1 endless
2 hassle-free
3 stands head and shoulders above all the others
4 common occurrence
5 drawbacks
6 are keen to
7 become intertwined with
8 at your fingertips
9 to take the drastic measure

Reading and writing: activity 3

Students write their summary about the advantages and disadvantages of the Internet using their notes from Reading and writing activity 2. This activity could also be done for homework.

Speaking

Students discuss the questions in small groups.

Alternatively:

Discussion carousel

These questions could be photocopied and cut up into sets of four questions. Students work in three groups. Each set is placed separately on a table. Students start at one table. Give a time limit for each set (e.g. 5 minutes). When the time runs out, ask each group to move clockwise to the next table, and so on.

What's the question?

Students work in pairs. Give each pair one question to answer and a strip of paper. Students write a brief answer to their question. Collect the answers and hand them out randomly so that each pair has a different answer. Students have to find which question was answered, agree or disagree with this answer and give their reasons.

Extra activity

Worksheet 1

Success and failure (idioms)

Activity 1:

Ask students to look up the idioms in an English dictionary and write them under the correct heading. Explain that we commonly use these idioms for a project/activity, a person, a film, or a company. You can divide the class into two groups. One group works on 'success' idioms and the other on 'failure' idioms. Check the answers and the meaning with the whole class.

Answers:

Success: to bring the house down; to work like clockwork; to go from strength to strength; to get off to a flying start

Failure: it doesn't cut the mustard; it was a flop; to be a dead loss; to take a nosedive; to be back to square one; to get off to a flying start

Activity 2:

Students work in pairs or small groups and play a board game. You will need a dice per pair/group and a counter for each student. Students move a counter round and talk, for about a minute, about the success or failure of the particular person/film/project, etc. Encourage students to use one of the idioms each time.

Project

Students work together in groups to research famous inventions. Have a list of some inventions ready. Research can be done for homework. Students compare notes and prepare a short talk for the class. Encourage students to cover the three main bullet points.

Alternatively:

Students can prepare posters about each invention and deliver a presentation.

Have a class discussion at the end (see the questions on page 108 in the Coursebook).

After the discussion about inventions, elicit what people buy online. Ask students to discuss what can go wrong with these things. For example, clothes – the wrong size; electronics – faulty; presents for friends and family – damaged packaging, long delivery times; downloads – being asked to pay the wrong amount. Remind students about the target audience and the appropriate style and register. For homework, students write an email to complain about a new product they have bought.

Features of the email:

- target audience – somebody we don't know, customer services
- style and register – formal letter/email (introducing the complaint, describing the problem(s) in more detail, asking for action to be taken)

Language focus

Linkers of contradiction

Analysis

Check students' understanding of the idea of contradiction. Draw their attention to the Key term box. Students then work in pairs and circle the linker in each sentence. They can use the questions in 'How do we use the linkers?' to help them.

Check answers with the class. Elicit the idea of two contrasting/contradicting ideas joined together.

Answers:

A Even though all these inventions are extremely important, not many people know about them.

B Research for an assignment is much easier from your own home. However, you often get distracted.

C The Internet is very useful for finding information. Nevertheless, sometimes the information is not accurate.

Students work in pairs / small groups and look through the reading text, 'And they said it would never work …'. They highlight the linkers of contradiction they find and discuss their usage.

Answers:

however / even though / in spite of / although

Each pair/group is then given one linker from the text and a big piece of paper to write their answers on. All groups rewrite the same two sentences ('I had a terrible headache' and 'I helped my friend with his homework' from the Coursebook) using their linker and make a poster for other students to see. Students should also answer the questions in 'How do we use the linkers?' – encourage the use of an English dictionary for this activity. Students look at examples of usage for each linker in the dictionary.

Check answers together. Each group shows their sentence to the class and explains the usage and punctuation. Help out where necessary.

Answers:

- *Although* I had a terrible headache, I helped my friend with his homework.
- I helped my friend with his homework *although* I had a terrible headache. *(followed by a subject and a verb)*
- *Even though (Used in the same way as 'although'.)*
- *Despite* having a terrible headache, I helped my friend with his homework.
- *Despite* the fact that I had a terrible headache, I helped my friend with his homework.
- I helped my friend with his homework *despite* the fact that I had a terrible headache. *(followed by a noun phrase)*
- I had a terrible headache *but* I helped my friend with his homework. *(Note that no comma is needed if the subject is the same in both clauses. In this case it is 'I'.)*
- *In spite of (Used in the same way as 'despite'. Note the use of the preposition 'of' with 'in spite'.)*
- I had a terrible headache. However, I helped my friend with his homework. *(Followed by a sentence that contradicts the previous sentence. It is often used at the beginning of the second sentence.)*
- *Nonetheless / Nevertheless (Used in the same way as 'however'.) The linker can also be placed between the subject and verb, e.g. … this, nevertheless/ nonetheless/however, was a failure.*

Practice

Exercise 1

Do this exercise with the class. Make sure that students use the correct punctuation.

Answers:

1 Despite the rain, I went for a jog. OR Despite the fact that it was raining, I went for a jog.

2 Although I was angry with her, I smiled.

3 The test was hard. However, I passed with top marks.

4 Rodrigo was tired but he joined us for a walk.

5 In spite of the fact that Marta has a lot of clothes, she keeps buying more. OR In spite of having a lot of clothes, Marta keeps buying more.

6 I can't cook. Nevertheless, I agreed to cook lunch for my best friend.

7 Even though it was very late at night, I phoned Gaby for help.

8 Despite the fact that I wasn't feeling well, I went to school. OR Despite not feeling well, I went to school.

Exercise 2

This exercise can be done as homework. Students spot common mistakes and correct them.

Answers:

1 In spite of <u>it was late</u>, I wasn't feeling tired. *(In spite of the fact that it was late, I wasn't feeling tired.)*

2 He'd been studying very hard. <u>Nonetheless he</u> failed the exam. *(He'd been studying very hard. Nonetheless/ Nevertheless, he failed the exam.)*

3 She had very little experience <u>although</u> she was offered the job. *(Although she had very little experience, she was offered the job.)*

4 Even though I don't like romantic <u>comedies I'm</u> going to see one with Nadia tomorrow. *(Even though I don't like romantic comedies, I'm going to see one with Nadia tomorrow.)*

5 Despite <u>of</u> the noise coming from the street, I fell asleep. *(Despite the noise coming from the street, I fell asleep.)*

6 I normally go to the cinema at the <u>weekend however this weekend</u> I'm going to the museum of unusual inventions. *(I normally go to the cinema at the weekend. However, this weekend I'm going to the museum of unusual inventions.)*

Activate your English

In small groups, students discuss the advantages and disadvantages of the inventions. Encourage the use of contradiction and other linkers. Do a few ideas together first.

Extra idea
Students could write a discursive article as a follow-up activity, using some ideas from their discussion.

Extra activity

Worksheet 2

Punctuation

Remind students about punctuation (capital letters, commas, full stops, question marks, apostrophes, etc.) and some common rules.

Students work alone, proofread the text and correct the mistakes in the passage. Then they check in pairs before checking with the class. If possible, project the text onto the board for the feedback session together.

Answers:

The object I **can't** live without is my mobile **phone**. Wherever I **go, I** take it with me. **I'm** in my late teens so I don't know what it was like when people **didn't** have any mobiles. How did they manage to **meet?** Everything must have taken a very long time. If I had lived in those **times, I** would have gone crazy. I know that people had phones in their **homes, but** what happened when someone phoned them and they weren't at home**?**

Mobile phones have speeded up things too. **Do** you need to meet someone or tell them **something?** You just phone them and a minute later **it's done**. **Nevertheless, I** feel we are losing the patience to do things slowly and enjoy the moment.

I got a really great smartphone from my brother **E**nrico. Now I also have instant access to the Internet. **Plus, my** phone doubles up as an MP3 player too. **I'm** really grateful to all the people who have brought us these technological advances. Thank you.

Listening

Pre-listening activity

First check students' understanding of the inventions on the list. Students discuss the questions and report back.

Listening: activity 1

Students listen to the six recordings and match each invention to the correct speaker. In pairs, students discuss which words were spoken that helped to identify the invention.

Answers:

- Speaker 1. MP3 player: *32GB, upload quite a lot of songs*
- Speaker 2. microwave: *cook, a cooker, reheating, not for serious cooking, nothing I cooked in it came out crisp*
- Speaker 3. e-book: *reading, novels, it's not the same as reading a real one, it comes with me in my handbag*
- Speaker 4. vacuum cleaner: *cleaning, carpets*
- Speaker 5. mobile phone: *contact, press the wrong button, phone someone*
- Speaker 6. contact lenses: *put them in, discreet, my optician, pair*

Extra invention: laptop

Listening: activity 2

Draw students' attention to the Study tip box (matching speakers, lexical links and implied information). Go through this Study tip box with the whole class.

Then students look at statements A–G. Explain any unfamiliar vocabulary. Students listen and match each statement to the correct speaker.

Note: if you want to do this exam-type exercise under exam-like conditions, omit the steps outlined in the two paragraphs above.

Answers:

- Speaker 1: B
- Speaker 2: G
- Speaker 3: D
- Speaker 4: C
- Speaker 5: A
- Speaker 6: F

Extra letter: E

Vocabulary 3

Attitudes and feelings

Exercise 1

Students work in pairs, look at Transcript 15 and find the words/phrases that mean the same as the adjectives/phrases in Exercise 1.

Answers:

Speaker 1:

- I didn't expect that: *I was really surprised*
- I was angry: *I was cross with …*
- I was discouraged: *I was put off by …*

Speaker 2:

- I was happy: *my friends were excited*
- I was disappointed: *It was a real let-down*

Speaker 3:

- I was very happy: *I was really thrilled*

Speaker 4:

- I was satisfied: *I was so pleased*

Speaker 6:

- I find it difficult: *I struggle …*
- I don't find it easy: *It's tricky for me*

Exercise 2

Students focus on four common adjectives of feelings and attitudes and think of some more synonyms for these. These could be idiomatic expressions too. Encourage the use of a thesaurus, which can be found online along with most common online English dictionaries. If time is limited, divide the class into four groups. Each group is given one adjective.

Alternatively:

Think of a list of synonymous words or phrases yourself. Divide the class into four groups and give each group a marker pen and a piece of paper. Each group focuses on one of the adjectives. Dictate the words/phrases in random order. Each group writes down only the words/phrases that are synonymous with their adjective. Check answers together. Encourage students to help each other and to notice stronger and weaker adjectives/phrases.

As a follow-up activity, students discuss what makes them … (+ adjective) OR what they find difficult.

Possible answers:

- Happy: *content, feel over the moon, ecstatic, delighted*
- Unhappy: *miserable, be down in the dumps, gloomy, depressed*
- Angry: *infuriated, furious, it drives me up the wall, irritated, mad*
- Difficult: *tough, challenging, demanding, heavy-going*

Draw students' attention to the two sentences (A and B) and discuss the difference in use between the two suffixes *-ed* and *-ing*.

Which suffix do we use to talk about somebody's feelings? *(-ed)*

Which suffix do we use to describe a situation, person, place or thing? *(-ing)*

Practise together:

For example, 'Why are you interested in English?' *(The grammar is interesting.)*

Exercise 3

This exercise could be done for homework.

Answers:

1 boring
2 fascinated
3 discouraged
4 relaxing
5 embarrassing
6 shocked
7 fascinating
8 disappointed
9 satisfying
10 terrified

Highlight the change in spelling – *satisfying* BUT *satisfied*.

Activate your English

Students work in pairs and discuss the bullet points. Encourage the use of a wide range of phrases for different feelings and attitudes.

Stop this activity after a few minutes and ask students to choose one of the topics in the box. Give students time to prepare. Students should talk for about a minute on the chosen topic without identifying which one it is. Other students listen and guess the answer. You can also set a few more questions before other students listen. For example, put a few question words on the board: *when, why, where, who with*, etc. Students write down the answers they hear.

Writing

Pre-writing activity

Students work in small groups and discuss their experience of losing things and answer the questions.

Writing: activity 1

Students read the exam-type question and identify the key information. Check that everyone has understood. Then put students into pairs, ask them to think of some ideas and make notes.

Writing: activity 2

Ask students how they plan and record their ideas before they start writing. Stress the importance of the planning stage before writing an answer (e.g. email, letter, article, etc.). Elicit the advantages of the planning stage. (*Thinking of ideas, the number of paragraphs, what information in each paragraph, making sure the content points from the question are answered.*) Discuss how long they would spend on it. (*Not too long – time limit in the exam, longer when doing homework*).

Students look at different ways of recording ideas and compare them. Discuss together which way students prefer and why.

Writing: activity 3

Students use their notes from activity 1 to write their answer. Encourage students to proofread their written work before handing it in.

> **Extra idea**
> This activity could be done as a collaborative writing task in class. Students write their answers in pairs or small groups.

Writing: activity 4

Students read the sample answer, underline the answers to the bullet points from activity 1 and discuss, in pairs, the organisation of the ideas in the text.

Answers:

- Say what you lost and where you lost it: *MP3 player, on the bus.*
- Describe what you were doing when you lost it: *We were chatting and I got off the bus without it.*
- Explain what you have learnt from the experience: *I realised how careless I am with my things and also how much I love my music. I can't be without listening to music for more than a day.*
- All the content points are answered, but in rather a disorganised manner. The paragraphs and the ideas in them need to be organised in a more logical order.

Writing: activity 5

Ask students to decide which ideas they would put in each paragraph. Most answers will be very similar, but allow variations if clearly and logically organised.

Suggested answer:

- Paragraph 1 – opening sentences: ask how your friend is / thank your friend / apologise for not writing / say why you are writing.
- Paragraph 2 – first and second bullets: say what you lost, where you lost it, what you were doing at the time. *(Each bullet point can be written as a separate paragraph if preferred.)*
- Paragraph 3 – say what you learnt from the experience.
- Closing sentences: (optional) invite your friend somewhere / say when you are going to see each other, etc.

Writing: activity 6

Ask students to look at the highlighted phrases and linkers in the sample email. Students choose one of the plans from activity 2 and write their answer. Encourage students to think about the organisation of their answer and use some of the expressions from the sample email.

When students have finished, ask them to swap their answers with a partner and check the organisation and paragraphs.

The writing stage for this activity could be done for homework.

> **Extra idea**
> The best written work can be photocopied for other students to keep. These can be compiled by students as their writing portfolio of sample answers.

Summary page

Can you remember …

Use one of the extra ideas in previous chapters for doing this revision activity. At the end ask students to assess their progress and decide what areas they need to revise more.

Answers:

- the words that mean: a) to decide not to use something right now, but maybe later, b) paper used for notes, c) a problem that stops you from being successful? *(a – to be shelved, b – scrap paper, c – an obstacle)*
- **three** inventions that were predicted to be unsuccessful, but became very popular? *(e.g. sticky notes, the telephone, shopping online)*
- the reason why the telephone was predicted to be a failure? *(They were thought to be unnecessary for companies that used messenger boys for communication purposes. William Preece thought it was a novelty that wouldn't last.)*
- what the missing words are from the following phrases? 'to stand … and shoulders above all the rest'; 'to have everything you need at your …'; 'to take drastic …' *(head; fingertips; measures)*
- what the phrases above mean? *(noticeably better than the rest; very near and ready to use; to do something extreme and unwanted, but necessary)*
- **one** linker of contradiction that is followed by a noun, **one** that is followed by a subject and a verb, and **one** that needs a comma? *(e.g. despite, even though, however, etc.)*
- what the mistake is in the following sentence? 'Despite <u>of it was raining</u>, we decided to go jogging.' *('Despite' is not followed by a clause, or a preposition. 'Despite the rain, we decided to go jogging.)*

- how to use 'in spite of', 'although' and 'however'? Think of three contrasting ideas for the use of mobile phones or computers, and make three sentences using these linkers. *(students' own answers)*
- **three** synonyms for 'happy' and **two** for 'angry'? *(possible answers: happy – excited, ecstatic, pleased; angry – upset, cross)*
- when we use the suffix *-ed* and when we use *-ing* with adjectives? *(-ed– feelings; -ing – to describe a situation, person, place or thing)*
- if the following suffixes are used correctly? 'I was really boring with the book. It wasn't particularly interesting.' *(bored)*
- what to do before you start writing? *(Students should read the question and highlight the main content ideas. They should also spend a short time planning how to organise the ideas and how many paragraphs they will need.)*
- when we use 'you'll never believe this' and 'that's why'? Make **two** sentences using these expressions. *(delivering unexpected news; explaining a result. Possible answers: You'll never believe this, but I've passed my driving test! I was exhausted, so that's why I decided not to go to the cinema last night.*)

Progress check

After completing the Summary page questions, encourage students to go back to the Objectives at the beginning of the chapter and assess their learning progress. Students should use the symbols suggested in the Progress check box. This can be followed up in tutorial time with individual students.

Chapter 8 – Worksheet 1

Success and failure (idioms)

Activity 1:

We often use these idioms to talk about the success or failure of a project, a person, a film, or a company. Can you put these idioms under the correct heading: success or failure?

- to bring the house down
- to work like clockwork
- it doesn't cut the mustard
- it was a flop
- to be a dead loss
- to go from strength to strength
- to take a nosedive
- to be back to square one
- to get off to a flying start

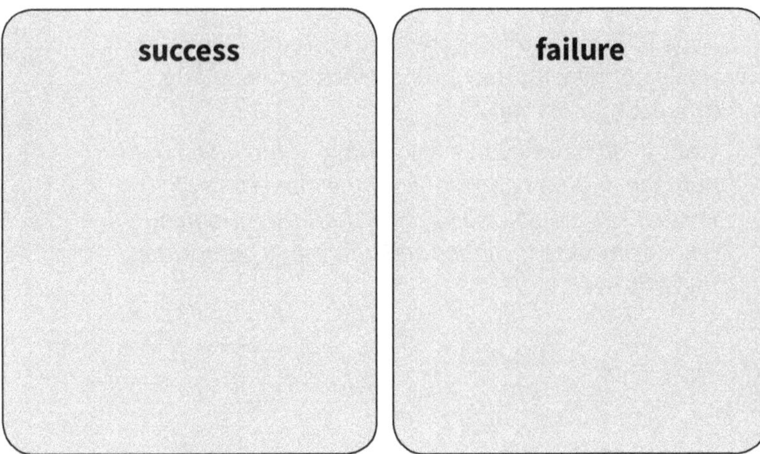

Discuss the topics using the success and failure idioms.

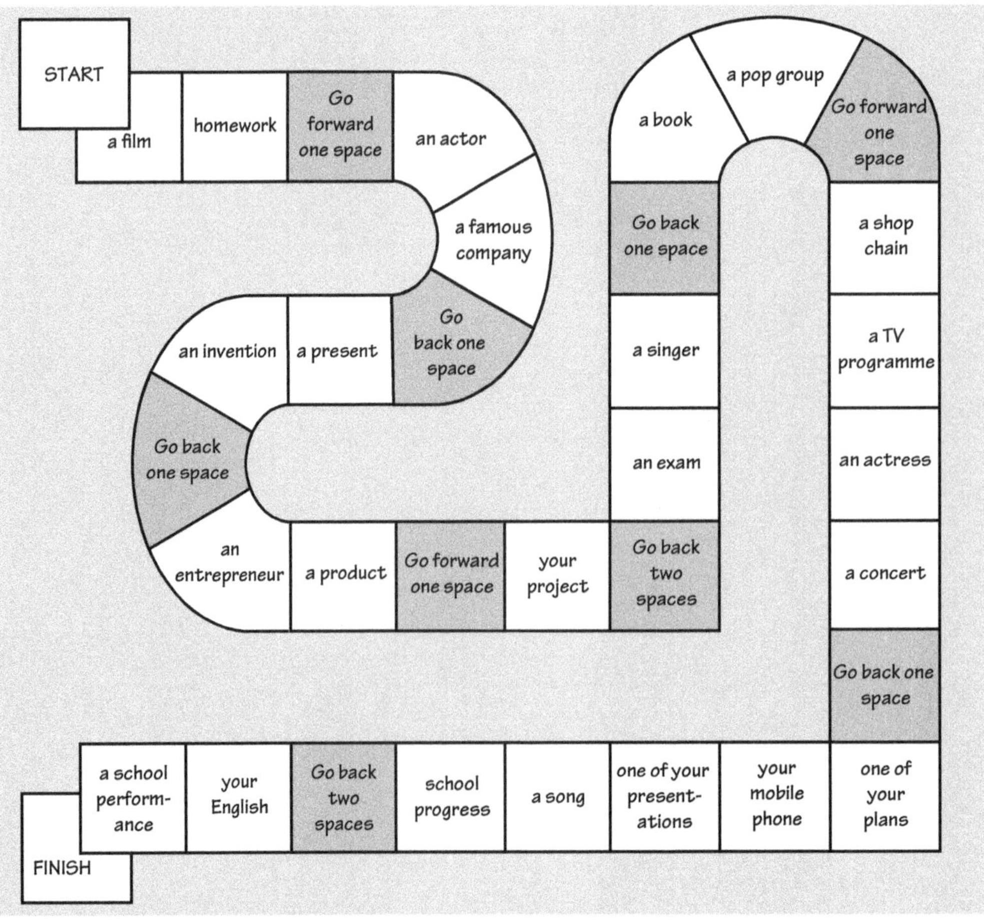

Chapter 8 – Worksheet 2

Punctuation

Can you correct the punctuation errors?

The object I cant live without is my mobile phone Wherever I go I take it with me. Im in my late teens so I don't know what it was like when people didnt have any mobiles. How did they manage to meet. Everything must have taken a very long time. If I had lived in those times I would have gone crazy. I know that people had phones in their homes, but what happened when someone phoned them and they weren't at home. Mobile phones have speeded up things too. do you need to meet someone or tell them something. You just phone them and a minute later its done Nevertheless I feel we are losing the patience to do things slowly and enjoy the moment.

I got a really great smartphone from my brother enrico. Now I also have instant access to the Internet. Plus my phone doubles up as an MP3 player too. Im really grateful to all the people who have brought us these technological advances. Thank you.

Chapter 9
Endangered species

Reading

Pre-reading activity

Students look at the pictures and in pairs answer the questions about the endangered animals shown in the pictures. Encourage a short class discussion.

Answers:

A *Sea turtle*
B *Mountain gorilla*
C *Bengal tiger*
D *Blue whale*
E *African elephant*
F *California condor*
G *Giant panda*

2-4 Students' own answers

Reading: activity 1

Remind students about scanning and what it is used for. Students scan the first paragraph and find the numbers. They read the relevant information to find what the numbers refer to. Don't let students read the whole paragraph. Encourage scanning reading techniques. When checking answers with the class, encourage students to use their own words.

Answers:

1. 30: three subspecies of tigers have become extinct in the past 30 years
2. 5000–7500: an estimate of how many tigers remain at present
3. 3200: the number of tigers still surviving in the wild
4. 100 000: the number of tigers at the beginning of the 20th century

Vocabulary 1

Students look at the highlighted words and guess their meaning. Do the first three together (see the guiding questions). Students then work in pairs and guess the meaning of the remaining words. Don't allow students to use their dictionary at this stage. Compare students' guesses with the whole class. If guesses differ, choose somebody to check in the dictionary and tell the class the correct meaning.

Alternatively:

Type up all the correct definitions and give each pair a copy. Students guess the meaning first and then find the correct definition on the list to see if their guess matches one of the definitions on the list.

Reading: activity 2

Students read the text and answer the questions. They compare answers in pairs before checking with the class.

Answers:

1. They are classified as endangered.
2. South China Tiger and Sumatran Tiger.
3. 20 years ago.
4. It was a popular sport.
5. A tiger's claw.
6. Its body organs.
7. By cutting down trees and polluting the atmosphere.
8. *Any two from:* they are good swimmers / they are good climbers / their ability to adapt.
9. The sale of all tiger-related products in China.
10. To double the number of tigers in the world.

Reading: activity 3

Draw students' attention to the table in the reading text 'Can they survive?'. Ask students to write a few more questions about the information from the table. Students then swap their questions and find answers in the table.

Reading: activity 4

Ask students to look back at the study tip about graphs and charts in chapter 6. Students then look at the graph and chart in this activity and answer the questions. For homework, ask students to prepare more questions either about the same graph and chart or ask students to bring more graphs for the next lesson. They prepare questions for other students to answer. Students can compete with each other to see who finds the correct answer first.

Alternatively: students prepare their own graphs / charts based on the information they find. The topic can be – the fastest animals in the world / the most endangered animals in the student's country / the most popular animals amongst students at the school, etc.

Answers:

1 bowhead whales
2 100 years
3 swans, parrots and elephants
4 cats
5 hamsters

TEACHING TIP

For practice in reading and writing, collect a variety of texts. For reading comprehensions, the texts can have subheadings (e.g. leaflets, information sheets, etc.). Students work in pairs. Each pair is given a different text. They read the text and prepare questions about it. Encourage students to use a wide range of question words (e.g. *what, what time, who, how many, why,* etc.). Two pairs then swap their texts and questions and they read their new text and answer the questions. When they have finished they check that they have the correct answers.

Encourage discussion about the topics/issues in each article. Students choose the topic/issue they are interested in for their discussion. They can also prepare a few questions to ask other students (e.g. 'What would you do in this situation?'). Students can discuss what they found interesting, shocking, uninteresting, or surprising, and what they have learnt from reading the article.

As a follow-up activity, students make wall posters with 'mind maps' of words connected to the topic they have read about.

Speaking

Students work in small groups and discuss the questions.

Alternatively:

Copy the questions and cut them up into strips. Each student has one question strip. Students mingle and discuss the questions.

Extra idea

The last question in the Speaking section can be used as a statement to write an article. Elicit students' opinions and write them on the board. Students choose ideas for and against and write an article for homework.

Project

Students work in groups. They choose one of the animals from the pictures in the pre-reading activity. Students research the animal for homework and find the information required in the bullet points. In the following lesson they compare the information with other students in their group. Then they prepare and give a short talk to the class. Encourage the use of visuals.

Other groups should take notes while listening to each talk. After they have listened to all of the talks, they decide which animal is in the greatest danger. Encourage a whole class discussion.

Students use their notes, and the information from all of the talks, to write a report on conservation projects. Students can research more information for homework. Before students write their reports, elicit why we write reports, who is likely to read them and what style and register is necessary. Students discuss in groups how they would organise their ideas and how many paragraphs they would use. Set the writing of the report for homework.

Features of reports:

Reports are written for someone in charge and need to be written in a formal register. Reports use headings, subheadings and bullet points to make it easier for the reader to locate the main information easily. The first paragraph introduces the aim of the report and how the information was collected. The middle paragraphs provide objective facts. The last paragraph contains personal suggestions or recommendations.

Extra activity

Worksheet 1

Word formation

Photocopy the worksheet or copy the table onto the board. Students write the eight words in the correct space provided. Students then work in pairs to complete the others. Check answers together. Ask students to mark the syllable stress and practise the pronunciation.

To listen to how the words are meant to sound, go to http://dictionary.cambridge.org and listen to the words being spoken.

Answers:

Noun	Adjective	Verb
extinction	extinct	–
captivity	captive	capture
prediction(s)	(un)predictable	predict
confinement	confined	confine (often used in the passive – to be confined to something)

controversy	controversial	–
abandonment	abandoned	abandon
denial	(un)deniable	deny
end(ing)	endless	end

Students then choose any five words from the table and write sentences with gaps. Each gap should represent one of the words that have been chosen. They read out the sentences to the pair next to them to see if they can complete the sentence with the missing word. Each time the word is a match, the pair gets a point. As a class, compare the number of points for each pair. Any pairs with all five points are the winners.

Encourage the use of an English dictionary for the word formation and to help students with writing gapped sentences.

Speaking and listening

Listening: activity 1

Introduce the idea of asking for clarification and delaying answering questions in discussions. Draw students' attention to the Study tip box. Students look at statements A–D. Check students' understanding of the four statements. Students listen to the four dialogues and match the statements to the correct speaker.

Students listen again and write down the correct phrase for each situation. If necessary, students can look up the phrases in the transcript.

Answers:

- Speaker 1: C – *We'll have to wait and see. Only time will tell.*
- Speaker 2: B – *I'd rather not talk about it if you don't mind.*
- Speaker 3: D – *Sorry, you've lost me.*
- Speaker 4: A – *Sorry, nothing springs to mind.*

Listening: activity 2

Students work in pairs. They look at the five extra phrases and match them to the correct situation.

Answers:

1 D
2 D
3 C
4 D
5 A

Pronunciation

Explain the idea of word stress in sentences (we stress the words that are the most important to the message we are trying to convey). Play the recording and ask students to underline the word that is stressed. Check answers with the class. Play the recording again and students repeat the sentences, practising the correct stress.

Answers:

1. Sorry, I'm not following.
2. Sorry, I didn't quite catch that.
3. It's too early to say.
4. Sorry, how do you mean?
5. Sorry, my mind's gone completely blank.

Speaking

In pairs, students make dialogues based on the situations given. Encourage the use of phrases from Listening activities 1 and 2. At the end, choose one pair to act out their dialogue for the class. Students listen for the phrases used and for other details. Ask them questions at the end of each dialogue. For example, Situation 1 – *What phrase did they use? How does student A get to student B's house?*

Language focus

Present perfect simple and continuous

Analysis

Ask students to read the sentences with a partner. They underline the present perfect simple and circle examples of the present perfect continuous.

Answers:

1. Three subspecies of tigers **have become** extinct in the last 30 years. *(present perfect simple)*
2. The number of surviving tigers **has been declining** dramatically for the past few years. *(present perfect continuous)*
3. This **has resulted** in the reckless poaching of tigers. *(present perfect simple)*
4. Humans **have also changed** the natural habitat of the tiger. *(present perfect simple – highlight the word order here when using an adverbial phrase)*
5. Some countries **have been trying** to save the remaining tigers for many years now. *(present perfect continuous)*
6. **I've never seen** a tiger in its natural environment, but **I've seen them many times** in the zoo. *(present perfect simple)*

7 **I've always liked** tigers. They're very graceful animals. *(present perfect simple)*

Then students answer the questions by deleting the wrong answers. When checking the answers to 'which tense', ask students to give an example from the selection of sentences.

Answers:
Underline the correct answer.

1 present perfect continuous
2 present perfect simple
3 present perfect simple
4 present perfect simple
5 present perfect simple
6 present perfect simple
7 present perfect simple

State verbs

Explain the meaning of state verbs – draw students' attention to the Key term box. Students work in pairs and circle all the state verbs. Encourage the use of the dictionary to check these.

Answers:

State verbs – *know, belong, love, hate, believe, own, want*

Practice

Exercise 1

Do this exercise together. Insist on students explaining why they need to use the present perfect simple or continuous.

Answers:

1 *I've known*
2 *I've been studying*
3 Tim *has been listening*
4 My sister *has always wanted*
5 *I've never liked*
6 *You've been running*
7 How long *have you been reading*
8 How many times *have you read*
9 How long *have you had*
10 *Have you had*
11 *I've bought*
12 *They've come … I haven't seen*
13 *He's been sleeping*
14 *I've overslept*

Exercise 2

Students first work on their own and complete the sentences with their own ideas. Monitor to check that students are using the correct tense. Check answers together. Students then tell their partner their sentences. They should use each sentence as an opening sentence and expand this into a dialogue with their partner. Give a few examples how to expand a dialogue (e.g. asking an additional question, showing interest, adding extra information, etc.).

Activate your English

The preparation for this task could be done for homework. Students think what they have done / have been doing in their life and put this information on the 'path of life' with some time expressions.

They then explain their 'path of life' to their partner. Their partner should ask additional questions.

For homework students can write this information as a short paragraph.

Listening

Pre-listening activity

Students answer the questions in pairs. Elicit a few answers from the class.

Vocabulary 2

Students check the meaning of the words before they listen to the recording.

Listening: activity 1

Encourage students to look through the notes and predict the type of answer for each gap. Students then listen and fill in the gaps. Play the recording twice.

Answers:

A numbers
B vulnerable
C 50 per cent
D Deforestation
E fatal
F famous people
G relocate
H volunteers

Listening: activity 2

Tell students that numbers are often tested in the listening. Play the recording again. Students should write down all the numbers they hear. They compare their answers in pairs. Go through the answers together and practise saying them.

Answers:
250 [animals left]

2500 [animals left]

10 000

50 [per cent]

10 [years]

20 [years]

20 [per cent]

1960s [year]

400 [birds]

10 000 [eagles]

Listening: activity 3

Students work in pairs. Each student writes down an example of a number from the list.

They read the numbers out in turns. Their partner has to write down the same number as heard. At the end students compare their answers.

Reading and writing

Pre-reading activity

Students work in pairs and discuss whether they are in favour of or against the idea of zoos. Encourage students to provide reasons for their opinions.

Reading: activity 1

Tell students that they are going to read an article and ask them in which paragraph they are likely to find the writer's opinion (**answer:** *the last paragraph*). Students read that paragraph and say whether the writer is for or against zoos. They also choose the best sentence as a summary of the last paragraph (**answer:** C).

Ask students if they agree with the writer's opinion.

Vocabulary 3

Students work in pairs. Each student looks at either the A or B list of words/phrases. Then they find a match with the correct word/phrase in the text (the words have been highlighted). Student A looks at paragraphs 1 and 2 and student B looks at paragraphs 3–5. Ask students to guess without using dictionaries.

When they have finished, they exchange their words. Check the answers together.

Answers:

Student A
Paragraphs 1 and 2

1 on a daily basis
2 aims
3 stand still
4 to put (severe) strain on
5 to spark controversy
6 to roam
7 to be kept in confinement

Student B
Paragraphs 3, 4 and 5

1 foliage
2 the chances are
3 endlessly
4 proponents
5 dwindling
6 abandonment
7 undeniably

Reading: activity 2

Students scan the text to find the pairs/groups of words. They find the connection between the words. Students tell each other what the connection is. Encourage paraphrasing. *(For answers students explain their meaning in their own words.)*

Writing: activity 1

Do this as a class activity.

Students look at the ideas from the previous activity and match them to the correct paragraph. Then they answer the questions. Tell students that when they are trying to think of ideas for their writing, they should write them concisely, as in Reading activity 2.

Ask students what they do before they start writing. Elicit a few ideas from the class and write them on the board. Don't tell the class whether these are good ideas or not at this point. Ask them to read the Study tip box to compare. Ask somebody to summarise again what should be done before students start writing.

Answers:

Introductory paragraph

1 'wealth and power', 'conservation and education' – to contrast the reasons for having zoos in the past and now; 'confinement' – to introduce the general opinion of zoo criticism.

2 Zoos have existed for a long time for a variety of reasons, but critics nowadays say that animals should not be kept in confinement.

3 No. Students' own suggestions. For example, *Should we therefore keep animals in zoos at all?*

Second paragraph

4 Against – 'roam, stand still', 'strain, chronic injury'.

5 A life in confinement in zoos doesn't suit elephants' natural lifestyle.

Third paragraph

6 'yet' – to introduce a contrasting idea.

7 For.

8 Animals threatened in their natural habitat – ivory, leather, meat; breeding programmes, survival; some animals need saving – circuses, natural disasters, injury and abandonment.

Fourth paragraph

9 Zoos with 'cement floors, metal enclosures' and 'a variety of habitats, toys and native foliage' – to contrast the difference in quality of zoos.

Concluding paragraph

10 Balanced – looks at positives and negative aspects of zoos – it is an objective view: 'repopulating, primitive treatment' and 'animal activists and zoo proponents'.

Writing: activity 2

Students should now apply what they have learnt in this section so far.

In small groups, students read the exam-type question and analyse it with their partners. Encourage them to underline the important information (e.g. topic, style, number of words).

Writing: activity 3

In the same groups, students think of some ideas together. They should group the ideas together and put them in the correct paragraph in activity 3. Compare students' suggestions as a class before they write their answers.

Writing: activity 4

This activity could be done as a group writing task. Give each group a big piece of paper and ask them to write out their answer. Stress that this is a group effort. Each student should have a different role in the group (e.g. one student dictates, one student writes, one student proofreads what has been written). When each group has finished, ask them to swap their answers with another group. Copy 'writing assessment' areas from Chapter 6 (Writing activity 2). Each group reads one answer and assesses their peers' written work. Monitor and help out where necessary. Discuss together students' strong areas and areas for improvement.

Writing: activity 5

Students choose one topic and write an article for homework. Insist that students also do the 'planning' stage. Collect this with their written work to check that students use this stage in their writing effectively.

Extra activity

Worksheet 2

Expressing points of view

Activity 1:

Ask students to complete the phrases with the correct word. Students choose the correct word from the box. Check answers with the whole class. Ask students which phrases are used to agree with a point of view and which phrases are used to object to a point of view.

Answers:

1 view *(oppose)*

2 most *(agree)*

3 favour *(agree)*

4 appalled *(oppose)*

5 understand *(oppose)*

6 circumstances *(oppose)*

7 necessary *(agree)*

8 simply *(oppose)*

9 agree *(agree)*

10 see *(agree)*

Activity 2:

Then students mingle and discuss the statements with other students. Encourage the use of the phrases. Give students enough time to discuss all the statements. At the end of this activity, elicit a few points of view with the whole class. For homework, students choose one statement and write an article. Alternatively, students write a letter to a friend about a pet they've had, or about their last visit to a zoo.

Summary page

Can you remember ...

Students work in groups and answer the questions. This could be done as a group competition. Award points for each correct answer. At the end ask students to assess their progress: what they can do well, what they need to improve. Ask them what they can do to be more successful. Encourage a short discussion.

Answers:

- and name at least **four** endangered species? *(for example, giant panda, blue whale, sea turtle, mountain gorilla)*
- what the opposite of 'in the wild' is? *(in captivity)*
- the meaning of the following words: *to diminish; poaching; to become extinct; to spot? (to become smaller [in number]; illegal hunting; when a species dies out; to notice)*
- **three** phrases you can use to ask for clarification? *(for example: Sorry, I'm not following; How do you mean? [informal]; Sorry, I didn't quite catch that.)*
- what information about verbs we can learn from a dictionary? *(if they are: state verb / action verb, regular / irregular, need an object / don't need an object)*
- the difference between a state verb and an action verb? (*State verbs can't be used in continuous forms; action verbs can be used in both forms in tenses: simple or continuous.*)
- which verb is **not** a state verb: *to love; to study; to believe; to know? (to study)*
- what the mistake is in the following sentence? 'I've been knowing him for three years.' *(I've known him ...)*
- what tense we commonly use with the following time expressions: for four months *(present perfect continuous)*; many times *(present perfect simple)*; never *(present perfect simple)*; since this morning *(present perfect continuous; there are instances when we could also use the present perfect simple – 'I haven't seen him since this morning' – this is more commonly used in negative sentences)*; always *(present perfect simple)*? Can you make a sentence with each of them? *(students' own answers)*
- **two** common reasons why animals become endangered? *(two from: changes to their habitat; poaching; introduction of alien species to the native species' habitat)*
- the words that mean: 'to work very hard'; 'a guess about something that may happen in the future'; 'easily hurt'? *(to work relentlessly; a prediction; vulnerable)*
- why the following pairs of words were used in the article about zoos: 'conservation and education'; 'roam and stand still'; 'toys and native foliage'? *(See article in the Reading and writing section.)*
- what you should do before you start writing? *(think of ideas, plan how many paragraphs, organise ideas in paragraphs)*

Progress check

After completing the Summary page questions, encourage students to go back to the Objectives at the beginning of the chapter and assess their learning progress. Students should use the symbols suggested in the Progress check box. This can be followed up in tutorial time with individual students.

Chapter 9 – Worksheet 1

Word formation

Put the words in the correct box: noun, adjective or verb. Then complete the table with the other forms of these words.

1 extinct	2 captivity	3 predictions	4 confinement
5 controversy	6 abandonment	7 undeniable	8 endless

	Noun	Adjective	Verb
1			
2			
3			
4			
5			
6			
7			
8			

Chapter 9 – Worksheet 2
Expressing points of view

Activity 1:

Look at the phrases expressing points of view and complete the missing words. Choose the best word for each phrase from the box below. Are these phrases used when you agree with something, or object to it?

simply favour view circumstances understand see most appalled necessary agree

1 I definitely oppose the .... that ...

2 I .... definitely support the way ...

3 I'm in .... of the idea that ...

4 I'm absolutely .... by ...

5 I'll never .... how ...

6 Under no .... should we ...

7 I feel it's absolutely .... that ...

8 I .... can't support the idea of ...

9 I couldn't .... more with ...

10 I'm extremely pleased to .... that ...

Activity 2:

Use the phrases to discuss the following statements.

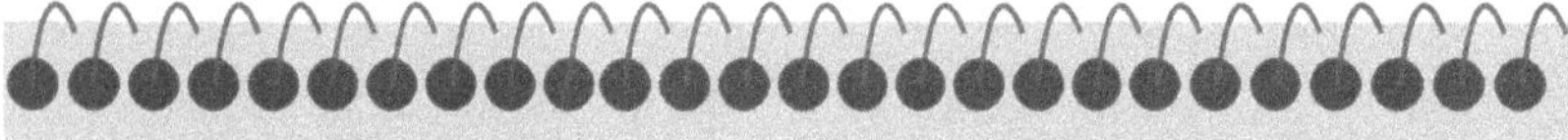

- Having a pet teaches children to be more responsible.
- Keeping animals in zoos is the only way of saving them.
- There should be more charities helping animals in need.
- Most zoos don't provide an adequate environment for their wild animals and the animals suffer as a result of this.
- If everyone became vegetarian, there would be fewer endangered species.
- Using fur in fashion should be banned.
- Humans are the most dangerous species walking the earth.

Chapter 10
Achievements

Reading and writing

Pre-reading activity

In small groups, students discuss whether they know who the women are, where they're from and what their achievements are. If you think they may be unfamiliar with the women in the pictures, photocopy the answers below and delete the names. Students match the achievements to the right picture and discuss whose achievement is the greatest, in their opinion. Encourage whole group interaction. Students compare their ideas.

Answers:

1. Florence Nightingale – improved health care and sanitation in hospitals; established nursing as a respectable job for women at the time. (England)
2. Michelle Obama – academic achievement (Harvard Law School); bringing community together (developed the University of Chicago's first community service programme); tackling child obesity (launched a campaign 'Let's Move!'); juggling two roles: mum and the First Lady. (USA)
3. Maria Sharapova – ranked world number 1 in tennis on five separate occasions in singles; managed to defeat Serena Williams. (Russia)
4. Zhang Ziyi – actress and model, spokesperson for Care for Children (a foster-home programme) and Global Ambassador for the Special Olympics (a sports organisation that organises competitions for adults and children with intellectual disabilities) and ambassador for other various causes. (China)
5. Marie Curie – discovered two elements (radium and polonium), awarded two Nobel Prizes for science, the first female professor at the Sorbonne University in Paris. (Born in Poland, lived and worked in France)
6. Maria Montessori – educator; attended a boys' school in Rome; became the first female doctor in Italy; fought for women's and children's rights; new method of teaching (focusing on each child as an individual, encouraging independent learning). (Italy)
7. Angelina Jolie – actress and UN ambassador for refugees. (USA)
8. Iman Mohamed Abdulmajid – model, actress, entrepreneur, pioneer in ethnic cosmetics (started a cosmetics firm producing difficult-to-find shades for ethnic women in 1994), various charitable work (e.g. ambassador for Save the Children); studied political science in Kenya; fluent in five languages. (Somalia)

Reading: activity 1

Students scan the text about Maria Montessori and find what the numbers / names of places refer to. Students compare in pairs before checking with the whole class.

Answers:

1. Maria Montessori was a doctor, a director of a school and a teacher.
   - Maria was born on **31st** August 1870.
   - Maria was **14** when her family moved to Rome.
   - Maria graduated with high honours from the Medical School of the University of Rome in **1896**.
   - **60** is the number of children from the slums Maria worked with.
   - By **1925** more than 1000 of Maria's schools had opened in the US.
   - The **60s** saw the return of Maria's teaching ideas in schools.
   - Maria's family moved to **Rome**; Maria attended a school there.
   - Maria's school, which followed her teaching method, opened in **the USA**.
   - **India** was where Maria was forced to emigrate during World War II.
   - **The Netherlands** was the country where Maria died.

Vocabulary 1

Divide the class into two groups, A and B. Each group looks up the meanings of the words in their list in an English dictionary. Monitor them to check the students can find the right meaning. Where more than one meaning is possible, encourage students to find the words in the text and guess from the context which meaning is correct. Then pair students up so that student A works with student B. Encourage students to explain the meanings to each other in their own words.

Reading: activity 2

Students read the text again and write notes under each heading. Encourage students to underline the information in the text.

Answers:

Difficulties Maria faced: *any two answers from: traditional ideas; opposition from her own father, teachers and male students; Maria also battled a lack of trained staff; Maria had to start teaching in appalling conditions; the Ministry of Education didn't approve of her work; the Ministry of Education denied her access to children in public schools; she was criticised; had to flee when World War II started.*

Children Maria worked with: *any two answers from: children from poor and disadvantaged families; children who came to the free clinics attached to the medical school; mentally ill children; young people from the slums; schoolchildren who were between the ages of one and six.*

Maria's achievements: *any three answers from: graduated with high honours; first female doctor in Italy; the improvement in her young patients; many of the children, after reaching adolescence, managed to pass the standard exams taken in the public schools in Italy; the children were immediately interested and their behaviour changed dramatically; her findings spread throughout Europe and the USA; by 1925 there were more than 1000 of her schools in America; two Nobel Peace Prize nominations; her teaching methods 'follow the child' are still used nowadays all over the world.*

> **TEACHING TIP**
> Remember that the information content is more important than the way it is expressed, and it must be written under the correct heading.

Writing: activity 1

Students write their summary using their notes from the previous exercise, or more ideas that they found in the text for their note-taking activity. Encourage students to use their own words and to use linkers and complex sentences.

> **TEACHING TIP**
> The content of the summary must be relevant, but accuracy of language is most important in this type of exercise. Students must not write over the word limit.

Alternatively:

This activity could be done as a group writing exercise. Students work in groups and agree on the points to be included in the summary. They write their summary on a large piece of paper and edit their work as a group. Choose one summary to show to the whole class for analysis and correction.

Writing: activity 2

Students read the sample summary and say what ideas are included. Ask students to guess the type of word that is omitted (i.e. articles). Students work in pairs and complete the gaps in the summary with the missing articles.

Answers:

1 an
2 the
3 the
4 a
5 the

Writing: activity 3

Students work in pairs and underline the linkers in the summary. They decide together why we use them. Elicit the correct answers and highlight how these are used: are the linkers followed by a noun, pronoun, noun phrase, or a clause? Are they used to start a sentence or to link two clauses together? Remind students about the use of commas after some of the linkers.

Answers:

The linkers are:

- whose – *relative clause*
- also/and/Moreover – *adding ideas*
- Despite this – *contradiction (followed by a noun / a pronoun / a noun phrase)*
- Last, but not least, – *sequencing, listing the last item*

Writing: activity 4

Students write another summary about the difficulties Maria had to face. Encourage the use of linkers used in the previous activity (*whose, also, and, moreover, despite this* and *last, but not least*). This exercise could be done as homework.

Writing: activity 5

Go through the bullet points and make sure students understand each point. Students then swap their summaries and assess their partner's answer. Ask them to put a tick next to the points that are done correctly, and a cross next to things that are missing from the summary. Students give each other feedback.

Extra activity

Worksheet 1

Linkers

Part A

You will need one set of cards for each group: this is a matching sentences activity (only cut up the right-hand part, keeping the left-hand part as one block).

In pairs, students match the correct halves. Check the answers and also check with students how each linker should be used (what follows, where it is placed and the punctuation). Ask students to use the first halves and complete the second halves with their own ideas.

Answers:

1 E
2 H
3 A
4 G
5 B
6 C
7 D
8 F

Part B

Copy the linkers and the discussion cards on two different-coloured cards and cut up. You will need one set for each group.

Students work in small groups. Set a time limit for the activity. Both piles of cards should be face down. The first student picks one discussion card and two linkers. The students have a discussion but have to use both linkers during the course of the discussion. After they've finished they should put the cards with linkers back (but not the discussion cards). They continue until they've talked about all the topics, or until the time runs out.

Speaking

Divide the class into two groups (or four if the class is too big). Each group is given one set of questions, A or B. If there are four groups, each set of questions is discussed by two groups. Give each group a time limit. Students discuss the points on their list. One student writes down what the group agrees on. When the time is up, ask students to move clockwise to the next table with the next set of questions. Alternatively, students can just pass on the question sets.

When all the groups have discussed both sets, encourage a class discussion. Choose questions where opinion is required for this.

Extra idea

1 Students can interview people from the older generation about their school days and prepare a presentation about the changes in the way we are taught.
2 Some of the questions in the Speaking activity could be used as prompts for an exercise in article writing.

Language focus

Narrative tenses

Analysis

Give students some time to read the paragraph. Students should then close their books and tell each other what they can remember. Ask a student to tell the class, encouraging others to add any missing information.

Ask students if they noticed the four mistakes in the text (***Answer***: *mistakes in tenses*). Students scan the text and underline the mistakes. In pairs they correct these mistakes (see A–D below). Ask four students to write their answers on the board. Encourage peer correction.

Answers:

A When I first saw him, he sat quietly at his desk and read something. *(… he was sitting quietly at his desk and reading something.)*
B I was sitting next to him and asking him in English what his name was. *(I sat next to him and asked him in English what his name was.)*
C He already studied at the school for three years when I started. *(He'd already been studying at the school for three years …)*
D Before meeting him, I only learnt the words 'Hello' and 'Thank you', but Yusuf taught me more. *(Before meeting him, I'd only learnt the words …)*

In pairs, students answer the questions 1–8. When they have finished, go through students' answers together to make sure they have understood the difference in the way we use past simple and continuous and past perfect.

Answers:

1 Past continuous – '… he was sitting quietly at his desk and reading something …'
2 Past simple – 'I sat next to him and asked him …'

3 Past perfect simple – 'Before meeting him, I'd only learnt …'
4 Yes.
5 No.
6 Johan singing.
No.
7 I came in.
Yes.
8 No.
No, she'd finished.

Practice

Exercise 1

Do this exercise with the whole class.

Answers:

1 was leaving / started
2 got / realised / I'd left
3 saw / knew / I'd met
4 entered / was laughing
5 had done
6 was flying / felt / I'd never flown
7 overslept / hadn't set
8 were / never liked
9 was shining / was enjoying / arrived
10 told / couldn't

Exercise 2

Students work in pairs and complete the sentences with their own ideas. Ask a few students to write their answers on the board. Encourage peer correction where necessary. Alternatively, students can write their answers for homework.

Exercise 3

Copy the words onto card and cut them up into sets, one for each group. Students work in groups. Ask them to close their books and put the cards in the correct order. Check the order. Students retell the story using the correct tenses. When they have the complete story, they write it down.

Ask each group to display their story. Students read all the stories and discuss which one is closest to the original story and what information was left out. Encourage class discussion.

Alternatively:

Instead of reading each other's stories, students can read them out loud.

The correct order:

Dubai / 11 years old / excited / run away / Yusuf / Egypt / quietly / his name / a house on fire / three years / Arabic / 'Hello' and 'Thank you' / beginners / fluent / miss

Activate your English

Students work in groups of three. Each student chooses one topic card and prepares a short talk. Encourage students to use narrative tenses in their talk. Then they tell the others in the group. The other students have to guess the topic.

Students can choose one topic and write a short paragraph for homework.

Extra activity

Worksheet 2

Narrative tenses – a day in my life I'll never forget

Each student has a copy of the worksheet. Tell students that their answers don't have to be true, but they must be grammatically correct.

Students should write one answer at a time and then fold the paper outwards so that the next question is at the top. They then pass their copy to the person sitting on their left, who does the same. Students continue until they have answered the last question. Then they put all the worksheets together and choose one. They work in groups and read out these stories. Each group then chooses the funniest or the most bizarre story and reads it out to the class.

For homework, students can write a new story which is true.

Listening

Pre-listening activity

Students work in pairs and answer the questions about different kinds of achievements and the difficulties people had to overcome.

Elicit a few ideas and opinions from the whole class.

Listening: activity 1

Students listen to six speakers and say what kind of achievement is mentioned for each person. Students compare in pairs and discuss which achievement they consider the biggest and the most important and why.

Check answers with the class.

Answers:

- Speaker 1: freed his country.
- Speaker 2: sailed round the world on her own.
- Speaker 3: helped others / worked for humanity.
- Speaker 4: has gained a lot of knowledge from life and can now offer useful advice to the younger generation.
- Speaker 5: published a book of children's stories.
- Speaker 6: looked after four children and had a job.

Listening: activity 2

Ask students to look at the list A–G. Make sure students understand the words. Students match the correct letter to each speaker. Play the recording twice. Students check in pairs before checking with the class.

If you want exam-like conditions, skip step one.

Answers:

Speaker 1: C
Speaker 2: F
Speaker 3: A
Speaker 4: G
Speaker 5: D
Speaker 6: E
Letter B is not used.

Listening: activity 3

Students listen again and write down the phrases that helped them to decide on the correct answer. If necessary, students can read Transcript 19.

Answers:

- Speaker 1: *he never gave up / many other people would have just given up, but not him / he just kept going / the determination to see his dream come true*
- Speaker 2: *no matter how scary this is / there is no place to hide, no place to run / you need a lot of courage*
- Speaker 3: *her work for humanity / she gave up all her material comfort to help others and put their needs before hers*
- Speaker 4: *he always has an answer to every problem or question / he gives me good advice based on his own experience / this amazing source of knowledge and information*
- Speaker 5: *always come up with extraordinary stories / fantasies*
- Speaker 6: *she managed to be so calm / she never complained*

Vocabulary 2

Phrasal verbs and other fixed expressions

Exercise 1

Students look at Transcript 19 and find the words and phrases that have the same meaning as the definitions in the exercise.

Answers:

Speaker 1

- to give up
- to start again from scratch
- to see your dreams come true

Speaker 2

- to keep your cool

Speaker 3

- to take up (a job)

Speaker 4

- to look up to
- to get through

Speaker 5

- to come up with (a story)
- to grow up

Exercise 2

Students work in pairs and match the correct halves. They guess which phrases are used to talk about success or failure. Divide the class into two groups. One group should focus on the phrases to talk about success, the other group on failure. They use an English dictionary to look up the exact meaning of the phrases. Monitor and help out where necessary.

Check the answers and understanding with the whole class.

Answers:

1 F (failure)
2 D (success)
3 H (success)
4 G (failure)
5 J (success)
6 A (failure)
7 I (failure)
8 B (success)
9 E (success)
10 C (failure)

Exercise 3

Students work in pairs and complete the sentences with the correct missing word, then have a short conversation with others using the sentences from the exercise. Encourage students to speak to as many different students as possible.

Answers:

1 look
2 given
3 come
4 went
5 failed
6 take
7 come
8 pass / flying
9 keep
10 success

Activate your English

Students work in small groups. Each student chooses one of the types of achievement and prepares a talk. Draw their attention to the bullet points. They should include all the ideas on the list. Encourage students to use the target vocabulary from this section.

Each student then gives the talk to the group. When they have finished, they should invite other students to ask questions about it.

Alternatively:

If time is limited this could be done as a writing exercise for homework. This could be read out at the start of the following lesson, followed by class question–answer time.

Project

Students prepare a presentation about a person they admire. They make notes which include relevant information to help them during the presentation. Encourage students to use pictures or a Powerpoint presentation.

Optional: After a few presentations, students have a discussion in groups or as a class, comparing the people mentioned in the presentations.

Writing

Writing: activity 1

Students read and analyse the question. Make sure the students understand the style, register, appropriate language choice, the content points and the organisation required.

Writing: activity 2

Students read the two sample letters and focus on the content points. They underline the answers in the text. Check together.

Answers:

Sample A

- say what your achievement was and why it is important to you: *I won a big tennis tournament / my self-confidence got a big boost.*
- explain how you prepared for it: *I'd been training really hard / I ate healthy food / I went jogging every morning.*
- describe the most difficult moment: *the weather – the sun was so bright / the temperature had reached the high twenties.*

Sample B

- say what your achievement was and why it is important to you: *I passed a very difficult test yesterday / it will help me to get to a good university.*
- explain how you prepared for it: *I studied hard for it / I went to the library every day.*
- describe the most difficult moment: *the time limit was very short / I had to hurry.*

Writing: activity 3

Students read the two sample letters again and compare how successful they are following the list. They decide what each student did, or forgot to do, following the ideas in the list.

Answers:

1 A, B
2 A, B
3 A
4 A, B. *Note that in sample B only simple linkers are used.*
5 A
6 A, B
7 A
8 A, B – some adjectives
9 A, B
10 A, B

Writing: activity 4

First draw students' attention to the Study tip box about how they can make their writing more interesting.

Students work in pairs and compare and analyse the two sample letters in terms of the language and vocabulary.

Check the ideas with the class. Get students to give more examples of interesting vocabulary from Sample A.

Answers:

1 Sample A: the vocabulary is more varied and interesting, the language is more natural-sounding and easier to read.
2 '*Speaking of which*' – to start a new idea that is related to something that has been said before, used to start a new paragraph / a new idea. *'I'd been training'* – gives more grammatical precision. 'Got a boost' – informal expression appropriate for this type of letter, gives more precision, expresses the idea more clearly for the reader.
3 No: the vocabulary in this letter is informal and therefore inappropriate for formal types of writing tasks.

Vocabulary 3

Informal expressions

Draw students' attention to the Study tip about using the appropriate register. Ask students for more examples of formal and informal expressions. Then ask students to look for more informal expressions that mean the same as the expressions 1–8.

Answers:

1 relieved
2 it's all over
3 I'm dying to … (+ infinitive)
4 a while back
5 my self-confidence got a big boost
6 to build up
7 boiling hot
8 fancy (+ *-ing*)

Writing: activity 5

Students work in small groups and rewrite Sample B. They should make the ideas more complex, adding more precise and varied vocabulary and grammatical structures. The letter should also have more paragraphs; there is no opening or closing paragraph. When students have finished, they swap answers and compare with another group.

Alternatively:

Each group can put up their answer on the wall. They read all the other answers and choose the most successful answer.

Writing: activity 6

This activity could be done for homework. Students write their own answer to the question in activity 1.

Summary page

Can you remember …

This can be done as a group competition. After the competition, go through the answers again to make sure everybody has the correct answers. At the end, encourage students to reflect on their progress and identify areas for improvement.

Answers:

- at least **three** of Maria Montessori's achievements? *(See answers in the Pre-reading activity.)*
- the meaning of the following: 'to battle something'; 'slums'; 'to flee'? *(to find something difficult; very poor, deprived areas in cities; to run away because of some danger)*
- **one** linker we use to add extra information and **one** linker to express contrasting ideas? Can you make a sentence with each linker? *(for example: Moreover – 'The staff were unhelpful. Moreover, no-one could give me the right information.' Despite – 'Despite feeling tired, I agreed to help him.')*
- what narrative tenses are? *(tenses we use when we talk about past events)*
- what is wrong with this sentence? 'When we had *(were having)* dinner, our neighbour had rung *(rang)* the doorbell.'
- how to use narrative tenses? Talk about what you did yesterday using narrative tenses. *(students' own answers.)*
- what these three phrasal verbs mean: 'to give up'; 'to get through'; 'to look up to'? *(to stop an activity; to manage to finish something; to admire and respect)*
- what the missing words are in these expressions? 'It was nothing to … home about'; 'It went … a storm'; 'I've passed my exams with flying …'. *(write; down; colours)*

- **one** more expression for success and **one** for failure? *(for example: a resounding success; it led to his downfall.)*
- how to make your writing more interesting? *(for example: varied vocabulary, varied grammatical structures, examples, linkers, etc.)*
- which informal expressions mean: 'to improve'; 'some time ago'; 'I really want to ... '? Can you make sentences with all three? *(to boost OR build up; a while back; I'm dying to)*

Progress check

After completing the Summary page questions, encourage students to go back to the Objectives at the beginning of the chapter and assess their learning progress. Students should use the symbols suggested in the Progress check box. This can be followed up in tutorial time with individual students.

Chapter 10 – Worksheet 1

Linkers

Part A

1	In spite of the bad news,	A	However, I'll give this one a go.
2	Despite being left-handed,	B	he spends most of his time at home.
3	I don't really like romantic comedies.	C	That's why my mum never buys any.
4	Although I told him many times,	D	I'm also hoping to lose some weight.
5	Because of his illness,	E	she seemed happy.
6	I'm allergic to citrus fruit.	F	What's more, you get to know new people.
7	I'm trying to get fitter.	G	he could never remember.
8	Travelling is fun.	H	he sometimes wrote with his right hand.

Part B

Linkers

What's more,	In spite of	Although	Because of
Also	Despite	That's why	However
What's more,	In spite of	Although	Because of
Also	Despite	That's why	However

Discussion cards

The person you look up to	Your favourite movie
There is not enough equality in our society	Who do you get advice from?
Health diet	Improvements needed to my local area
The advantages and disadvantages of travelling by car	The ways we can protect the environment
What is your country famous for?	Keeping fit
Where do you get information from?	How should children spend their free time?
Modern technology in your everyday life	My local community

Chapter 10 – Worksheet 2
Narrative tenses – a day in my life I'll never forget

Where were you and when?
What was the weather like? Describe what was happening around you.
Were you alone? What were you doing?
What happened?
How did you feel?
What were the people around you doing at the time? What else was happening around you?
What did you do next?
How did it all end?
How do you feel about it now? Why?